WHAT THE HELL ARE YOU DOING?

ARE YOU DOING?

*Smart and Easy Ways to Fix the
Mistakes You Make with Your Money*

KEN WEBER

with GENE WALDEN

GREENLEAF
BOOK GROUP PRESS

Published by Greenleaf Book Group Press
Austin, Texas
www.gbgpress.com

Distributed by Greenleaf Book Group

For ordering information or special discounts for bulk purchases, please contact Greenleaf Book Group at PO Box 91869, Austin, TX 78709, 512.891.6100.

Design and composition by Greenleaf Book Group
Cover design by Greenleaf Book Group
Cover image ©iStockphoto.com/TPopova

Publisher's Cataloging-In-Publication Data

Weber, Ken, 1947-
    Dear investor, what the hell are you doing? : smart and easy ways to fix the mistakes you make with your money / Ken Weber with Gene Walden. — First edition.

    pages ; cm

    Issued also as an ebook.

    1. Finance, Personal. 2. Investments. I. Walden, Gene. II. Title.

HG179 .W43 2015
332.678   2014943903

ISBN 13: 978-1-62634-161-6

Part of the Tree Neutral® program, which offsets the number of trees consumed in the production and printing of this book by taking proactive steps, such as planting trees in direct proportion to the number of trees used: www.treeneutral.com

TreeNeutral®

Printed in the United States of America on acid-free paper

14 15 16 17 18 19   10 9 8 7 6 5 4 3 2 1

First Edition

Dedicated to Neela.
The $30 "engagement ring" I bought in 1972
was the best investment I ever made.

CONTENTS

INTRODUCTION

This book is personal. No one told me to write it. No one promised to read it. I've written it because I needed to write it. It's from the heart. I can't keep witnessing all the mistakes good people make without at least trying to help.

This book is for *you*. Do you think that's a silly statement since I don't know you? Think again. I do know one thing about you—I know that you picked up this book because you must have some interest in money matters. And I know that *everyone* makes investing mistakes—even if they don't invest! (*Not* investing is almost always a mistake.)

Small investors make mistakes. Big investors make mistakes. New investors screw up, and highly experienced investors do lots of dumb things too. This is absolutely true—I could fill an entire book just citing all the examples of sophisticated investors kicking themselves for making boneheaded decisions.

If you felt a jolt when you first read the title of this book, great! This book is written as a wake-up call. As president of a registered investment advisor firm since 1987, I am privy to a constant stream of personal financial information, and I am continually amazed by the questionable decisions intelligent and otherwise successful people make with their investments.

That's why after years of doing this, I can say with near certainty—this book is for *you*.

A doctor who, in her professional life, would never dream of "trying something different" with one of her patients might very easily slide into such a foolish approach when handling her own portfolio. A carpenter who never fails to "measure twice and cut once" in his daily routine might do something impulsive in the stock market in an attempt to reap a quick fortune.

Don't kid yourself. All professional and vocational lines blur in any attempt to profile the investors who make the mistakes you'll read about in the pages that follow. The sabotaging of one's own portfolio is a thoroughly democratic venture.

This book is therefore written for cardiologists and carpenters alike—and for disappointed, unsuspecting investors everywhere who may have committed, or will commit, any or all of the following blunders:

- Sinking hard-earned money into a "hot tip" from a friend
- Buying a stock because you read an advertisement
- Failing to diversify your assets
- Missing big gains while waiting for the "right time" to invest
- Micro-managing your portfolio
- Completely ignoring your portfolio
- Buying an annuity without fully understanding its costs
- "Playing" the futures market with your kids' college fund

Are any of these familiar? This list is just a start; a full inventory of common investing errors goes on and on. Maybe you've made some of these mistakes. Maybe someone near and dear to you has made one or more of them.

Any of these mistakes can, at first blush, seem innocent enough. But once you understand the fallacy behind each of the common land mines discussed in this book, you'll be able to turn your portfolio around for the better.

And although I succinctly reveal the things you should do, you may wonder why I've chosen to concentrate on investing mistakes. Why focus on negatives—on those things you *shouldn't* do? Why not just come clean, and let you know *how* to invest so that you can get on with your busy life?

The answer to that is easy . . .

If you clear away all the mistakes, smart, rational investing is not terribly difficult.

On any given day, you can walk into your local bookstore and find dozens of books that tell you how to invest. In fact, you can locate hundreds of them right now by clicking on Amazon.com. This is not one of those books. I have no desire to throw my hat into a ring overcrowded with volumes of magic recipes that allegedly show readers how to score a windfall. Like the latest fad diet books, if those "recipes" for investment success actually worked, you wouldn't see new ones popping up every week. The advice in those books is sometimes good, sometimes misguided, and often too difficult to implement. In fact, sound investing is very much like changing your eating habits—once you strip away the bad stuff, reaching your goal becomes reasonably easy.

Besides, such advice changes from year to year, or even from week to week.

Over the three decades of my financial career (and I've been a stock market geek since I was a teenager), I've seen the so-called conventional wisdom on various types of investments swing this way and that. What had been accepted as dogma is suddenly upended by a new research paper.

Here's something most people don't realize: there is a river of financial information published every single day. Literally thousands of journals, white papers, magazines, newspapers, and blogs spew out facts, near-facts, and opinion. And much of it is published precisely because it counters previous conventional wisdom.

Even if you allow that each argument has merit under certain circumstances, how are you supposed to arrive at the *true* wisdom? And is arriving at that answer ultimately going to make you any money? Or is the effort even worth your time?

You'll read more about this later on, but for now suffice it to say, if the perceptions of the medical establishment were as scattered as the investment community, we might expect to wake up tomorrow morning with our livers on the wrong side of our bodies.

Before we get started, you should realize that just as there are no magic pills to help you lose weight permanently, there are no quick fixes that will make you rich in a few months. I'm not going to send you running to the Toronto Stock Exchange to chase down mining stocks, or to NASDAQ in search of the "most promising" IPO. I'm not going to recommend any one sector of the economy over the other.

I won't do that because the markets are in a constant state of flux, and more importantly, that's not what this book is about.

While I eventually will offer my prescription for how to structure your nest egg, this is essentially a book about what *not* to do with your hard-earned money. And for most investors I've met, that's the better advice.

Since your investment mistakes are inextricably tied to your outlook and how you think about your money, I begin with a discussion in chapter 1 on "Great Expectations." In my professional life, I've seen too many investors derailed by impatience, gullibility, hubris, impulsiveness, and by placing their confidence in all the wrong sources. If you approach your investments with reasonable expectations, you can avoid these destructive approaches.

But now that I've grabbed your attention with a promise to reveal your investment mistakes, the very last thing I want is for you to think of me as the one who merely chides you about all the wrong things you do with your portfolio. The very best ball players, the finest musicians, and the most successful executives all need a coach at one time or another in their careers. In that spirit, I want to be the investment coach at your side, not the cranky money guy on your back. Best to think of me the same way you think of a golf coach who implores you to make a subtle adjustment to your swing, or the executive coach who helps you tweak your five-year plan.

The bad habits I discuss throughout this book may seem tough to cure. But the good news is that with a reasonable amount of knowledge, patience, and discipline, you can make a big difference over time. Altering your destructive investment habits is probably easier than you may have expected.

One of the finest investors in the world, Warren Buffett, has sagely observed that, "it's not necessary to do extraordinary things to get extraordinary results." Believe those words.

You do not need to be as sophisticated as Warren Buffett, nor spend eight hours a day researching your investments. But you must be informed. Financial success is within your reach if you take smart steps towards your ultimate goals.

So please, Dear Investor, take the title of this book to heart, and as you read each chapter, I hope you will ask yourself: "Indeed . . . what the hell *am* I doing?"

Part 1

GETTING ON TRACK

Chapter 1

GREAT EXPECTATIONS

*Investing should be more like watching paint dry or watching grass
grow. If you want excitement, take $800 and go to Las Vegas.*
—*Paul Samuelson, Nobel economist*

It was 1999, the height of the tech stock bubble, when a new client called my office and uttered the following words: "Ken, I'm not greedy. I'll be happy with an average 15 percent annual return over the next ten years."

Great expectations, indeed. But the client wasn't stupid—he was a young physician—and he wasn't alone. At the time, some tech stocks were climbing 15 percent in a *good week*. So how could 15 percent in a year be an unreasonable expectation? In fact, many neophyte investors, jaded by their sudden success, would have laughed at a meager 15 percent.

But they wouldn't be laughing long, as the high tech sector began one of the biggest free falls in stock market history. Those weekly 15 percent gains soon became double-digit losses.

I often think about that conversation with the young physician, and the countless misperceptions, misguided conclusions, and ill-conceived notions that have tripped up millions of well-intentioned investors.

That's what we'll examine in great detail throughout this book.

Successful investing begins in the mind. It's a thought process. It's how you think about money, what you expect of it, and how you go about making your money work for you. In the end, your investment success is inextricably intertwined with your character and emotional make-up—and your ability to avoid the self-deceptive reasoning and delusional logic that often sabotages the best laid plans of many investors.

Fortunes can be made and lost through the assumptions investors make about their money. Reasonable expectations can set the stage for a coherent, prudent, and ultimately successful investment life.

But investing is a long and treacherous process. It involves not just one decision but potentially hundreds. You can't go through life without making some mistakes. But if you can minimize those mistakes through sound, rational decisions, you can maximize your investment success and, ultimately, your wealth.

It's a game of probabilities. If you can make more good decisions than bad, you become more likely to finish ahead of the pack. Where do you start? By learning to recognize some of the most common and destructive biases investors fall prey to.

BEHAVIORAL FINANCE

Investing, in very simple terms, is "seeking to maximize economic wealth." But studies in behavioral finance have demonstrated that investors routinely let their emotions and biases get in the way of sound investment decisions.

Most mental mistakes in investment practices are derived from mental shortcuts that cause us to make systematic mistakes. Worse yet, most investors are not even aware of these mistakes, so they continue to make them. Here are some of the most common biases; which ones can you relate to?

- **Fear and greed.** Emotions cause you to flee a bear market and plunge head first into a bull market, acting directly counter to the investment adage "buy low, sell high."
- **Overconfidence.** You have an inflated view of your ability to invest successfully.
- **Hindsight bias.** Investors I talk to have a bad habit of "predicting" the past, as if it was obvious what was going to happen—when the reality is it's never obvious in advance what is going to happen to the market.
- **Data mining.** That refers to the misguided practice of extracting patterns from random market developments to predict the future. In thirty years of investment management, I've learned one thing about predicting the market—you can't do it!
- **Anchoring.** That's the practice of mentally locking in a stock that has become irrelevant. It doesn't matter that a stock you bought at $30 is now trading at $10. It's no longer a $30 stock. Embrace that reality and realign your approach accordingly.
- **Mental accounting.** In your mind, you may be doing much better than what you're actually doing on paper. It's human nature to fool ourselves into thinking we're doing better than we actually are.
- **Status quo.** We have a natural aversion to change that can get in the way of successful investing. If things aren't working, we need to be able to recognize that and make the necessary changes to rectify it.

Now that you're aware of these common investor traps, your challenge is to avoid these biases in order to pursue a more coherent and successful investment process.

COMMON RATIONALIZATIONS

When things do go wrong, investors also have a natural tendency to rationalize those failings and blame their misfortune on sources or forces beyond their control. Here are a few of the most common investor justifications when things go south:

  a. It isn't my fault. The economy is in recession.
  b. It isn't my fault. Most investments of this sort (small stocks, emerging market stocks, long-term bonds, whatever) are doing poorly right now.
  c. It isn't my fault. My broker recommended that I make this investment.
  d. It isn't my fault. I got the idea from my brother (uncle, friend, coworker, cab driver).

Notice in these rationalizations it's either an *outside force* or *someone else* responsible for you losing money. In all four hypothetical instances, though, you're letting yourself off the hook.

These four *thinking traps* snag even seasoned investors. And as you work your way through the succeeding chapters, you'll discover a few additional thinking traps. In each instance of investor mistakes, you'll notice that it was created by a corresponding mistake in the investor's thought process.

WHEN A LOSS IS NOT A LOSS

From time to time I hear an investor say—after they've checked today's prices, of course—something to the effect of "I lost $20,000 this month" or worse, "I lost $5,000 today!"

There are two problems with such logic.

First, raw numbers mean little. Context is everything. What percentage of the entire portfolio does that represent? A drop of $20,000 would be 20 percent of a $100,000 portfolio but only 2 percent of a million dollar portfolio.

Second, one has to consider the real meaning of volatility vs. loss.

In my profession, we are prohibited from implying a guaranteed return. But we can guarantee one thing: volatility. It will always be a part of the market. As J. P. Morgan replied when asked to give his prognosis of the stock market, "It will fluctuate." That's essentially the definition of an open market—constant fluctuation. Supply and demand, among other factors, keep share prices in constant flux.

So if you are going to have money in the stock market, some days—make that *many* days—you will have "losses." But they are paper losses. They can only become real losses (or as your accountant would say, realized losses) when you actually pull the trigger and sell.

There's another type of perceived loss that also is common, and wrong. It's known as "opportunity loss." As in "I lost $250,000 by not investing in Google."

You can substitute the name of any company stock here. Certainly every age has seen its share of stellar stock performers. And feel free to substitute any amount of money. So if you're comparing notes (losses) with someone a few decades older than you, he might top you in the conversation by claiming: "Oh yeah? Well, I lost $10,000,000 by not investing in Wal-Mart."

The fact is, we've all piled up millions of dollars of "opportunity losses" by not investing in Microsoft, Google, Apple, Amazon, and any other stock that has experienced exponential growth. Opportunity loss regret is a perfect example of one of the behavioral finance traps I mentioned earlier—hindsight bias. In hindsight, we all should have invested in Apple stock in 2003 when it was trading at $13 a share (split-adjusted). It seems so obvious today, but if it really was obvious, why did so many of the sharpest minds on Wall Street—with all of their market experience and in-depth research—choose to ignore the stock? Simple answer: it wasn't that obvious.

What I am urging you to do, Dear Investor, is to let go of the pernicious thinking that blames market forces and other people for your investment mistakes, and to stop dwelling on the phantom dollars you mistakenly thought you lost.

RAISE YOUR HAND IF YOU THINK YOU CAN BEAT THE MARKET

Often when I speak to groups of investors I ask, "How many of you work with an investment professional?" Many hands go up.

Then I ask, "How many of you believe your investment pro can beat the market?"

Almost invariably, the same hands go up.

And when speaking one-on-one to investors over the years, it's clear that many folks believe professionals in the finance game ought to be able to beat the market. But here's the thing: unless you live in Garrison Keillor's fictional Lake Wobegon, "where all the children are above average," it's a mathematical impossibility for everyone to beat the averages.

It seems to me that many investors think of the stock market as some sort of mysterious "thing" out there somewhere, run by unknown forces. This thing, they assume, has a life of its own, and so they believe that anyone who studies the market long enough, or who understands it deeply enough, can surely beat the market.

But here's what's so widely misunderstood—the stock market averages are nothing more than an amalgam of all the buys and sells. And who does most of the buying and selling? It's the major investment professionals—mutual funds, college endowments, insurance companies, foundations, pension funds, etc., along with thousands of brokers and advisors buying and selling for their clients. Put in simplest terms, the stock market averages are a daily report card on the activities of "the big boys" (and girls) who control, directly or indirectly, trillions of dollars.

So if the market (let's use the Standard & Poor's 500 Index) rose one percent today, that means, in a very broad sense, that there was a little more interest in buying than selling today. Conversely, you can say that when the S&P 500 Index falls by one percent there are slightly more folks who wanted to sell than buy. (This is a highly simplified definition of market movements.)

You cannot know what the averages will do tomorrow, but you do know, assuming you got past fifth grade math, that for any given day roughly half the investment pros who move the market will be above the average, and roughly half below. And that same math logic applies to the performance for the week, month, year, or decade.

Well, actually, the odds of any one particular person beating the market are slightly less than 50 percent, since the market averages are simply theoretical entities, with zero expenses, while everyone else has to pay to play.

SETTING REALISTIC EXPECTATIONS

What should you expect from your investments? What should be considered realistic expectations and acceptable returns?

"Success" might be the most indefinable concept in investing. To the most aggressive investor, success means a penny stock that doubles overnight. To the retired pensioner, finding a local bank that offers a CD paying an eighth-of-a-percent-higher interest might bring a warm glow of contentment.

Wherever you fall in the spectrum, you must not allow yourself to get hung up on the returns of the most prominent stock market indexes—in most years the majority of professional investors do not match the returns of the Dow Jones Industrials or the Standard & Poor's 500. And if the pros have a hard time beating the indexes, it's clear that you, as an individual investor, are not likely to do better.

In any case, the big-name averages would be relevant to your results only if investing were a competition. It's not. Your purpose in stock market investing is to make a decent profit. *Whether someone else made more than you is irrelevant to your ultimate goals.* There will always be some people making more than you. And no matter how badly you may do, you can also be certain many people did worse.

After a few years, the most important criterion for measuring investment success is not complicated: Did you make more than you would have if you stayed in the safest investments? In other words, did you get paid for the risks you took?

Before you began your stock market investing, did all your money sit in bank accounts? If that's the case, then anything you did that returned more than bank rates spells success.

On the other hand, many investors fool themselves into thinking they've done better than they actually did. They focus on the winners in their portfolios and conveniently downplay the impact of the losers. That's human nature. We all do it, but it works against our long-term goals.

To know you've attained true investment success you must summon up the courage to take a cold, dispassionate look at your total investment picture. Some software programs allow you to input all your transactions and can then spit out an "internal rate of return." Most investors, however, have to settle for a seat of the pants estimate of their portfolio's performance.

If the sum of all your pluses and minuses leaves you with a rate of return higher than the safe investments, you're a success. If you beat inflation, you're a success. If you beat any of the stock market averages, you're a success. If you showed a gain during a period when the averages lost money, you're a success. And if by dint of luck or brilliance you achieved all these goals, luxuriate in your success—but never become so complacent that you think success is part of your nature. Over the years, you will experience both pain and gain, but with discipline and patience you will become a successful investor.

On the other hand, if your investment career has been a succession of disappointments and ill-fated decisions, you've come to the right place.

This book will open your eyes to the most common mistakes investors make in managing their money, and it will offer positive suggestions to improve your investment success. While it's important to identify the behavioral and psychological tendencies that may be standing in the way of your success, this is a book about improving your financial situation, not one about regrets.

The chapters are organized to be read consecutively from beginning to end, or scanned by the busy investor eager to zero in on her own situation. I understand that you might be busy and prefer to scan for a topic relevant to your current situation, but I urge you to eventually go back and read the entire book after you've concentrated on the chapters that are most pertinent to your experiences.

Remember: this book is *not* an ivory tower exercise based on esoteric academic research. Far from it. Every mistake and misstep you'll read about in the following pages is one I've seen time and time again from real investors. Real people. Smart people.

This book is your inoculation against making those same mistakes yourself.

Chapter 2

WHY DO YOU THINK THAT WAY?

Five Mental Mistakes to Correct Before You Invest a Penny

With our thoughts we make the world.
— Buddha

Most investment mistakes begin with our own faulty thought processes. We have biases, skewed notions, and emotional roadblocks we're not even aware of that get in the way of a rational investment approach. This chapter takes a look at some of the critical mental mistakes investors make in their investment process—the rationalizations, misapprehensions, and outright lies you tell yourself—in order to help you avoid costly decisions in the future that could sabotage your long-term investment plan.

MENTAL MISTAKE #1. THE IMPULSE TO ACT NOW ON YOUR ONE BIG INVESTMENT OPPORTUNITY

With investing, there is no such animal as "one big opportunity." Not the current price of gold, not the latest tech wonder stock, not your brother-in-law's burgeoning car wash business in downtown Seattle.

None of it! While it's true that you have to move off the dime and do something if you want to see your portfolio grow, you're deluding yourself if you think—or hope—you can pull off a lifetime's worth of growth with one or two big hits.

Successful investing is a process carried out over time. In a dynamic economy like ours, opportunities pop up with regularity—even during a recession. (In fact, the best opportunities often come during a recession when markets are depressed and stocks are "on sale.") Depending on prevailing market conditions, opportunities may be more or less robust, and they may present themselves with more or less frequency. But they do present themselves many times over a lifetime. It may take some education or some reliable professional help for you to recognize them. But they're there, and with patience and persistence, you'll uncover enough good opportunities to build a substantial retirement portfolio.

In other words, you don't need to roll the dice on one big opportunity. It's risky, it's irrational, and it's absolutely unnecessary. It's also impulsive and ill conceived.

As I have told many clients over the years: *Investing is a marathon—not a sprint.* So check your now-or-never mentality at the door. The stock market is a place to get rich slowly. What you're looking for is not an occasional miracle or hot tip, but an investing methodology you can use to build your portfolio over the long haul.

MENTAL MISTAKE #2. FOCUSING ON DOLLARS, NOT PERCENTAGES

"Ken," the panicked new client said to me over the phone, "I just opened my monthly statement and I lost $5,000!"

Well, first, he would have "lost" that money only if he had sold at that exact date, the closing date of the statement. But more to the point—is $5,000 a lot or a little?

I don't mean to be glib. Sure, five grand is real money. But what is the context of that money? Let's assume he is forty-five years old, has a good job with a great retirement plan, and that together we decided that he should be fully invested in the stock market. Let us also assume that his account was $200,000 at the beginning of the month. In that case, the "loss" of $5,000 represents a 2.5 percent decline. A one-month decline of that size is well within the normal range of stock market gyrations.

But even that does not tell us the full story.

Now let's assume further that the Standard & Poor's 500 Stock Index dropped 3 percent during the month. Suddenly we see that his account did well when compared to its benchmark. But the panicked investor did not realize that because he looked at the raw dollar figure, not the percentage.

Over the years, I have had many conversations with my clients on this topic, and sometimes they don't realize that the amount of money that caused them to lose sleep was less than 3 or 4 percent of their portfolio. Focusing strictly on a dollar amount, whether for a gain or loss, is almost always a futile exercise.

When it comes to your investments, the only way to make an intelligent, apples-to-apples comparison is to use percentages.

And always be aware of the context of your investments—what your specific goals are and especially what the overall market is doing. You are not investing in a vacuum.

The fact is, to become truly comfortable investing in the stock market you have to reach the mindset that volatility comes with the territory. There will be bad days, bad months, and yes, even bad years. It's all part of the ongoing cycles of the stock and bond markets. Expect it, count on it, and, in fact, be prepared to take advantage of it by investing more when the market swoons. Warren Buffett said: "Unless you can watch your stock holding decline by 50 percent without becoming panic-stricken, you should not be in the stock market." Now 50 percent is more than even I would be comfortable with, and declines of that magnitude are extremely rare. (And you only "lose" that money if you sell.) But with the right mindset, you can face any market decline with the resolve and realization that despite the inevitability of volatility, over the long-term the stock market has always trended up. We cannot make an absolute guarantee of that for the future, but history certainly indicates that the odds are on your side.

MENTAL MISTAKE #3. LETTING YOUR EGO DICTATE YOUR INVESTMENT DECISIONS

Your ego can sometimes get in the way of sound investment practices—particularly when you are dealing with an investment sales person who is well trained at appealing to your ego to sell you an investment that may not be in your best interest.

Let me share a story that was related to me by a former precious metals broker. I am not recounting it here to disparage the precious metals field, because the same story could have originated from a stock brokerage house, a firm that sells REITs (real estate investment trusts) or, for that matter, many organizations that sell investments to the general public.

Here is his story: "For two years of my five-year employment with a precious metals house in the 1990s, I worked on the busy trading floor in earshot of another broker with a very captivating phone personality. I'll call him Barry Barton. Through lively phone conversations, Barton was regularly able to persuade investors of means, without ever having met them, to wire hundreds of thousands—sometimes millions—of dollars to our firm.

"Occasionally Barton could pull off his magic in a single phone conversation. But more often, it took him a series of phone conversations with an investor to rake in the money. During one particular run of phone exchanges, I got to listen to Barton's end of his phone interplay with a successful orthopedic surgeon from a noted hospital in the Midwest. Barton was working hard to persuade his surgeon-prospect to invest in the silver market, which was then priced "attractively" at around $5 per troy ounce. Pieced together from what I heard from Barton's end of the conversation and what

Barton told me afterwards is this account of how their terse dialogue went down one particular morning.

(Barry Barton = BB; The Doctor = Dr):

BB: Good Morning, Doctor.

Dr: Morning, Barry. What's silver doing this morning?

BB: It's hovering around the $4.98 level—primed for a breakout. If you're serious about this, Doctor, I wouldn't wait.

Dr: What do you recommend in terms of an initial investment? I don't want to start too high.

BB: I'd recommend starting at the $100,000 level.

Dr: Forget it; that's much too high!

BB: C'mon! Really? For you, $100,000 is chump change, Doctor.

Dr: Absolutely out of the question! Forget it.

BB: Suit yourself.

BRIEF SILENCE

BB: Doctor, I know you have to go. But may I ask you a quick question first?

Dr: Yes, make it quick. I have to get ready for surgery shortly.

BB: Of course. I simply wanted to ask you whether General Practice doctors make a lot of money.

Dr: That's a strange question. But if you must know, that field is at the low end of the pay scale for physicians. Why do you ask?

BB: That's what I thought. Just before you called, a GP called this morning and took a position in the silver market for $200,000. As you might imagine, I was a bit surprised.

Dr: Hmmm . . . interesting.

BB: I thought so.

Dr: We'll talk soon. Take care.

Does it come as any surprise that the surgeon did in fact phone back the very next morning to let Barry Barton know he just happened to find "a spare $200,000 lying around," and he wanted to use the money to take a starting position in the silver market?

Your ego can be a powerful distraction from making intelligent decisions about your investments. You need to take your ego entirely out of the equation and focus on your lifelong financial plan. Investing is not a competition of clear-cut winners and losers—it's a long-term process that requires a series of well-planned, unbiased decisions.

MENTAL MISTAKE #4. BELIEVING YOU CAN MAKE UP FOR LOST TIME BY INVESTING MORE AGGRESSIVELY

Falling behind on your long-term investment goals can certainly be a cause for concern, but you can compound the problem by adjusting your strategy to try to make up for lost time.

If your lifetime goal is to average, say, 6 to 7 percent on your invested money, there's a decent chance you can achieve that through a practical, persistent investment program. But if you fall behind in your investment savings program and you suddenly decide you need to shoot higher to achieve your goals—say 15 percent per year—you are probably headed for trouble.

The problem is that your chances of earning double-digit returns over many years are extremely unlikely. I personally know of no money manager who, using any sort of normal mix of stocks, bonds, or mutual funds, can claim a long-term return in the 15 percent per year range. And if any advisor, mutual fund, or hedge fund does achieve that kind of return, you can be sure they are using highly aggressive, high-risk tactics.

As you probably realize, the higher your investment goals, the greater the risks you'll have to take to achieve those goals. It may mean buying stocks that are more speculative or high-yield, high-risk bonds that are more likely to face default. The more risks you take as an investor, the greater your potential gain, and also the greater your chances of failing.

Speculative stocks and high-yield bonds may give you the potential for greater returns, but only if you can pick them right every time. Unfortunately, neither you nor any other investor on the planet can successfully pick high-risk investments with any consistency.

They're high risk for a reason, and the more speculative investments you add to your portfolio, the more chances you give yourself to fail. And when you bomb on a speculative investment, if you placed too many eggs in that basket, the consequences can be devastating.

After a few failed investments, your total return will be far worse than it would have been with a prudent and reasonable investment selection process. So instead of making up for lost ground, you've fallen even further behind.

There are better ways to play catch-up with your investment goals. You can become more frugal, spending less and saving more in order to pump up your investment portfolio. You can also work longer. Instead of retiring at sixty-two or sixty-five, you might decide to keep working either at your current job or as a consultant or contractor. Even taking on a part-time job after you've retired from your full-time career can help you pad your nest egg in order to achieve your long-term goals.

Obviously, the best way to assure that you'll have the money you need to finance a comfortable retirement is to begin your investment program as early in life as possible and to continue to contribute throughout your lifetime.

Just don't become complacent. I've seen dozens of articles in the financial press that offer a scenario similar to this: If a young person could manage to save $50,000 by the age of twenty-five, and simply invest that sum in a stock or mutual fund portfolio, with a reasonable return of 8 percent per year, by age sixty-five—forty years later—that $50,000 would have grown to about $1 million.

Sounds great, right? Problem is the inflation-adjusted value of $1 million forty years from now—based on a 3 percent inflation rate— would only be about $300,000. Not only that, but how many twenty-five-year-olds could have socked away a cool $50,000—especially if they had college costs to cover? And chances are, if you're reading investment literature, you're probably well past twenty-five anyway, so that train has already left the station.

A better approach is to make a concerted effort to put away a set amount of money each month to invest for your retirement. If you start your savings program at age twenty-five and can earn 7 percent on your investments, you could invest as little as $417 per month in order to reach $1 million by age sixty-five. If you start at thirty-five, you'd need to invest $880 a month; at forty-five, you'd need $2,032 per month; and at fifty-five, you'd need $6,038 per month. But, again, keep inflation in mind. By the time you reach sixty-five, a million dollars won't have nearly the same value that it has today. But without question, the sooner you begin, the better your chances of having a suitable nest egg by the time you reach retirement.

MENTAL MISTAKE #5. FAILING TO LEARN FROM YOUR MISTAKES

Investing magnate Sir John Templeton had some very succinct but powerful advice for investors: "The four most dangerous words in investing are 'this time it's different.'" Self-deception is one of those shortcomings that always seem to bedevil *someone else*. Yet if that one trait weren't so ubiquitous, many more people would be successful at investing. Undaunted, those who pride themselves on being immune to self-deception are the ones who keep at it: a penny stock here, a momentum stock there, an errant tip there . . . *ad nauseum*.

OK, Dear Investor, it's time to pause here and, um, take stock.

Maybe you take the attitude of "damn the losses; keep rolling the dice; baby needs a new pair of shoes!" Or maybe you feel that, regardless of what happened last time, next time really will be different.

It won't be.

STAND UP STRAIGHT AND FACE THE MUSIC

If you are willing to admit that you are, in fact, prone to self-deception, or you know you've succumbed to any of the mistakes in *thinking* we've discussed in these first two chapters, let me strongly suggest you take the following steps:

- **Make a plan to invest.** More importantly, put your plan on paper (or on your hard drive). Write it down. Our mistakes in thinking—particularly self-deception—are much easier to catch when we commit them to "paper." In chapter 5, we go into detail about putting together your financial plan of action.
- **Enlist the services of a professional.** And I don't mean just *any* professional. At some point, you'll feel compelled to make an interesting choice. Should you seek investment guidance from a licensed stockbroker or a registered financial advisor? I recommend you choose the registered financial advisor. I'll let you know why later in the book.
- **Keep reading.** Several of the mistakes we've already discussed may seem all too painfully familiar to you. But once you recognize the mistakes you've already made, you can avoid making those same blunders again in the future.

Every investor stumbles. And the more years you spend in the world of investing, the more times you will stumble. No one bats a thousand in the stock market.

Chapter 3

FIRST, DO NO HARM

Not So Fast—It's Your Money We're Talking About Here

Sometimes the best investments are the ones you don't make.
—*Donald Trump*

You're probably familiar with that phrase *do no harm*. It expresses a time-honored principle of emergency medical treatment, which states that, under certain circumstances, it's better for a physician to do nothing instead of jumping the gun with a specific procedure or medication.

Most educated Americans are painfully aware that despite ready access to up-to-date technology and the very best training, the doctors who treat them occasionally make mistakes. That's the risk of taking action. And it's also why the cardinal rule of medicine is to "do no harm." Instead of jumping into action, a doctor must first consider the options carefully. It is that type of planning and careful execution that increases the success rate of their procedures.

Investors would be well-advised to take the same approach with their investment portfolios. First, do no harm. Take a deep breath. Think.

I've seen it again and again—investors rushing to do something because of a snippet of conversation at a party, a howling sound-bite from a TV talking head, an end-of-the-financial-world warning inside a direct mail envelope that screams with urgency, or any of the other myriad drivers of investor irrationality.

Don't sabotage your portfolio with rushed decisions and impulse purchases. Take the time to research and weigh every decision, to be as sure as possible that the investment you are about to make is appropriate for your overall portfolio. Just like physicians and their patients, taking any kind of risk when you don't yet know the odds or understand the stakes of the game is foolish and dangerous.

THERE'S NO SHOT CLOCK IN INVESTING

The professional basketball players of the NBA have twenty-four seconds to drive the ball up the court and take a shot. If they fail, the ball goes over to the other team. So the closer the shot clock gets to expiring, the more desperate the offensive team is to shoot the ball—and it seems the less likely they are to make it. As a result, just about the entire forty-eight-minute game is played at a furious pace, with both teams racing up the court and running quick plays to try to get a man open before the shot clock expires.

Fortunately, there is no shot clock in investing. So-called once-in-a-lifetime opportunities appear, amazingly, many times in a lifetime. But a lot of investors play the investment game as if they have a twenty-four-second shot clock to beat. Cash burns in their pocket.

A comment I've heard repeatedly from novice investors is, "I have some money lying around; I want to do something with it." My response to that line of thinking is to always ask the simple question, "Why?" After leaving a perceptible silence, I'll follow up with, "How?"

To your credit, if you have money lying around, that means you've been frugal enough to save some money and wise enough to realize that you did not need to invest that money immediately.

Speed is not a positive attribute in investing. In fact, my experience has been that those investors who trade the most tend to do the worst over the long term. Investing will always be a game of patience. It requires a well-conceived strategy. Spend some time to plan out your investment strategy and determine the best use of that money, and then begin your strategy slowly and thoughtfully.

Every dollar you add to your portfolio should be invested with a certain purpose. Your entire investment portfolio—including your 401(k), your house, your stocks, bonds and mutual funds, your insurance products and annuities, your real estate, your gold, silver, and jewelry—should all fit comfortably together like a carefully constructed jigsaw puzzle.

SPEED KILLS

When Facebook went public in 2012, millions of investors decided to throw their money at the stock, hoping it was going to be the next Apple.

As you may recall, Facebook stock moved up briefly on its opening from $38 to $42—and most got their shares near that peak price. But it quickly began to sink, ultimately hitting a low of $17.55 a share, primarily because the market started to feel that the stock was more hype than muscle. (As I write this, in late 2013, the stock has rebounded nicely.) But was there really a valid reason for millions of investors to buy Facebook stock? Did that purchase really have a purpose and a place in their overall portfolio? Probably not. It just felt like the right thing to do; the hoopla was deafening.

For most of those who bought Facebook, it was a poorly researched decision based on hype and emotion. And most of the time, decisions based on hype and emotions don't work out very well.

Truly, a large number of initial public offerings fall back to earth after their early run-up. Most spurted up on the offering, but ultimately dropped back below their offering price in the days or weeks following their IPO.

Facebook dropped just over 50 percent from its offering price to its fifty-two-week low, making it a typical example of IPO mania.

And of course, there have been plenty of emotion-driven investments that have fared worse than heavily hyped IPOs. Timeshares, jewelry, most artwork, penny stocks, foreign real estate, and just about any big investment deal put together by your cousin, uncle, or brother-in-law stand a good chance of being poor investments. Only rarely would any of those investments have an appropriate place in the portfolio of a typical investor.

When you invest, invest thoughtfully, and for the right reasons. There's no rush, no time clock. Allow time to research and consider your options. Just, please, Dear Investor, do no harm.

AN INCONVENIENT TRUTH

Here's some simple math to tell you why you don't want to make a dumb mistake. I can tell you that many folks do not understand this at first.

If your investment drops 50 percent, you then need that investment to go up 100 percent just get you back to even.

For the math challenged, let me show you. You have $1,000. You invest in, oh, say, um, Facebook on its opening day. After a while it has lost 50 percent of its value and now your investment is worth only $500. That $500 now has to double—meaning it has to increase by 100 percent—for you to get back to the original $1,000. Guess what? Not too many investments go up 100 percent, at least, not in a short time. A sharp drop is a deep hole, a steep hill to climb.

It's simple, devastating math. That's why I say first, do no harm.

Chapter 4

QUICK AND DIRTY TIPS

The Seven Most Common
Boneheaded Mistakes Investors Make

*Coaching is nothing more than
eliminating mistakes before you get fired.*
—Lou Holtz

To paraphrase Coach Holtz, investing is nothing more than eliminating mistakes until you make a new one. If you invest, you make mistakes. That's a given because there are endless iterations of gaffes you can make as an investor. And just when you think you've seen them all, you'll stumble over another one.

There's not much I can guarantee, but I can pretty much say with certainty: the longer you invest, the more mistakes you'll make. The key is to learn from your mistakes, and then stop making them.

Or even better, learn from others.

In this chapter, I'll discuss seven of the most common stock market mistakes to avoid. Chances are, through a lifetime of investing, you'll experience enough miscues, miscalculations, and missed opportunities on your own without adding these seven ill-conceived strategies to the list. How many of these "learning opportunities" have you already had the misfortune of experiencing?

1. CHASING PERFORMANCE: THE MONEY MAGAZINE SYNDROME

Too many investors pick up *Money* magazine or *Barron's* or some other publication that has a scoreboard of mutual fund performance, and then blindly throw money at the funds at the top of the rankings.

I know about this because in my early years I was one of those investors.

To me, those scoreboards are a cruel hoax. They provide little or no context for you to make a decision for your long-term portfolio. So Fund XYZ was the top performer for the past month, six months, year, or three years. Now what?

You need to consider many other factors. What was the overall market doing during that period? When the market is weak, "defensive" funds will rise in the rankings, but those same funds will drop in the rankings when the markets recover. And the opposite is true— when markets are strong, aggressive growth funds tend to shine, but they can hurt you the most when markets reverse course.

Then too, you need to consider how the political landscape, foreign and domestic, affected the stock and bond markets. What economic forces contributed to the performance of the market, and will those same forces still be a factor this year?

The published rankings of the "hot" funds tell you none of those things.

Nor do they tell you if the manager who was at the helm of a top-ranked fund is still guiding the ship.

Twice a year, Standard & Poor's publishes its "S&P Persistence Scorecard" to analyze the staying power of mutual fund performance over consecutive and overlapping time periods. The question the study tries to answer is whether the top mutual funds continue to provide the best returns over a many number of years.

In short, they do not:

> Very few funds can consistently stay at the top. Out of 703 funds that were in the top quartile as of March 2011, only 4.69 percent managed to stay in the top quartile over three consecutive twelve-month periods at the end of March 2013. ("Does Past Performance Matter? The Persistance Scorecard," Standard & Poor's, July 2013)

The results of that study are no surprise to seasoned mutual fund investors. What you see there is a market phenomenon known to math-minded folks as "reversion to the mean," which simply means that in spite of the ever-present cyclical volatility of the market, stocks and stock funds ultimately tend to revert to the market averages over time.

In other words, a hot sector won't stay hot forever. Whether it's medical stocks, military stocks, consumer stocks, or energy investments, at some point, that hot sector will become overvalued and slow down until the other market sectors begin to catch up.

There are other factors, as well, that tend to dilute the performance of a fund. The publicity that top-rated mutual funds receive tends to attract millions of dollars from new investors. As the assets under management increase, the fund typically becomes more unwieldy to manage. With $200 million of assets under management, finding and tracking a small portfolio of promising stocks should be very manageable. But if the assets under management balloon to say, $2 billion, everything changes. The larger a mutual fund grows, the more difficult it becomes to manage successfully and the more likely it is to revert to the mean—or even fall below the average returns of the mutual fund universe.

There is another Wall Street practice that tends to skew the performance numbers. Poorly performing funds are often liquidated or merged into another fund, which makes it seem that the mutual fund universe performs better than it actually does, since the worst funds—those that are put out of their misery—are not included in the rankings. This is what's known as "survivorship bias" and it traps unknowing mutual fund investors by causing misleading performance rankings.

Here's still one more trap for the performance chasers.

You look at a chart that shows annualized performance for the past three, five and ten years. In each period, the fund shows a better number than the S&P. That's good, right? It clearly means that you would have done well just about any time during that past ten years.

Not necessarily.

That fund may have languished for nine years, and then suddenly had a spurt over the past year—or even just the past few months.

As a result, ALL the time frames now look good. Most people don't realize that those performance time frames merely take the price-per-share on a current date (adjusted for any dividends or distributions) and compare it with the adjusted price on the same date three, five or ten years ago. In other words, those stats are snapshots of where the fund was back then, and where it is now, with no mind paid to what happened in between.

It can be extremely misleading.

Then there is the problem of Chasing the Market. We see it over and over: after a strong rebound in the stock market, headlines appear saying things like "Money Flowing into Stocks at a Fast Pace." Hope trumps both logic and a carefully structured strategy. American investors, year after year, want easy answers and quick results, and year after year, millions of them buy when the headlines scream "Dow Jones Industrial Average Sets New High," and then they sell when the headlines are nothing but bad news. Yes, they buy high and sell low. (We will look at this phenomenon in greater detail later on.)

It happens every market cycle. Investors pile onto the current hot funds and end up getting burned.

2. FOLLOWING HOT TIPS

Famed investor Jim Rogers said, "Get inside information from the president and you will lose half of your money. If you get it from the chairman of the board, you will lose all your money."

And you could go to jail. Acting on inside info is illegal. See: Stewart, Martha.

A hot tip is legal but almost always suspect. Where do you get hot tips? From the newspaper or the investment talk shows? That's a tip shared with hundreds of thousands of other investors. In other words, it's not much of a tip.

Or, do you get your hot tips from your friends, your neighbors, or your taxi cab driver? Consider the source. Where did your source get her tip? Chances are that tip came from a pipeline of questionable sources you have no way of verifying.

What about your broker? They're famous for hot tips. Does she have an occasional hot tip for you? Hmm . . . where would that tip be coming from? Again, consider the source. The motivation behind that "tip" may be to generate commissions. After all, your broker has dental bills and kids in college, and he or she likes a nice vacation now and then. That's the good scenario. Among the thousands of brokers out there, some surely will have darker motives, and you will never know. Addictions, gambling problems, messy divorce settlements—brokers are not immune from the same failings found within the general population.

Plus, sometimes brokers are encouraged to push a stock that the brokerage company holds in inventory and wants to unload. Again, you would never know. But even if the recommendation is legitimate, how "hot" is the tip? Your broker is probably one of hundreds or thousands of brokers in the company pushing the same hot tip, and you're one of hundreds of clients on your broker's list. You may be way down near the bottom of the food chain. By the time that tip gets to you, it could already have been offered to thousands of investors before you, so any benefit you might have gotten from buying the stock is long gone.

If you trade stocks, please don't rely on hot tips. Analyze each of your picks carefully, and make your decisions to buy or sell a stock based on sound research rather than on the advice of others.

Later in the book I will explain why I prefer mutual funds over stocks, but even with funds, don't buy merely because someone has given you a tip, hot or otherwise. You need to do your homework for any investment.

3. BEING OVER-DIVERSIFIED OR UNDER-DIVERSIFIED

Diversification of your investments is vital. You simply must spread your risk. But many investors build portfolios that are either too diversified or not diversified enough.

Put all in your eggs in one basket, and you can get rich. It's a gamble, but some people find the stock or mutual fund that explodes upwards. Keep all your eggs in that basket, and over time, it becomes more and more likely that you will be eating an omelet.

The ideal diversification would be to own a mix of stocks or mutual funds that give you exposure to a broad range of market sectors. It can be dangerous to load up your portfolio with just a handful of stocks, or many stocks from just one or two sectors of the market.

The most common case of under-diversification comes with individuals who own too much of their own company's stock.

You may work for a wonderful company—a company you truly believe will flourish for many years to come. But what if it doesn't? This scenario has happened to millions of investors. The company they work for hits a bump in the road. The stock drops, layoffs ensue, (and that could include you!) and they are suddenly holding a portfolio full of free-falling company stock.

Or worse yet, your company could go out of business entirely, leaving you with no job and a portfolio full of worthless shares of the company stock.

In some companies, retirement plans are tied to the company stock. Company stock may automatically be added to your retirement portfolio on a regular basis. Or you may have a chance to buy your company stock at a discount to the market, which encourages you to continue to pack your portfolio with your company stock.

That may be fine. Just be sure you don't overload your portfolio with that one stock. It's fine to make the company stock a part of your portfolio, but make sure you are well diversified with stocks or mutual funds that represent a broad range of industries.

On the other hand, maybe you're one of many investors who are actually too diversified.

As an advisor specializing in mutual fund investments, I have seen countless new clients who come to us with many dozens of mutual funds in their portfolio. Doing this defeats the purpose of mutual funds, because by buying so many funds you are basically just buying the market. You likely would have been better off just buying a couple of index funds for lower fees—and you and your accountant would have far less paperwork!

Many of those funds will be holding the same stocks, so while on paper you seem to be well diversified, there is a good chance you are not. If you want to own more than one fund in the same category (blue chip funds, for instance), you should make sure there is a logical reason to own them. For example, if the fund managers use different strategies for buying and selling the stocks in their funds, it might be worth it to own those funds to counter-balance each other under varying market conditions.

For most investors it makes little sense to hold more than a dozen different mutual funds. That is over-diversification.

4. BUYING ON PRICE, NOT VALUE

Price is what you pay, value is what you get.
—*Warren Buffett*

When you or I shop for a car, refrigerator, or just about any other consumer item, we all want to feel we've got a bargain. You'd like to buy that item for a price below its market value—and, in the case of investments, sell it at a price above its market value.

Those opportunities come along repeatedly in the stock market, but novice investors often pass them up when they become more concerned about movements in the price than in the true value of the stock.

Or they believe that the actual price of a stock tells them something. I have met investors who proudly inform me that they only buy stocks priced at $10 a share or less. They think they are being clever. They're not.

The right approach is to do your research and determine a fair intrinsic value for the stock. When the price falls below that value, it's an opportunity to buy. When it rises above the value, that's when you think about selling.

Then, too, I often hear about investors who buy a stock primarily because it's going up in price, and then they sell primarily because it's going down—with no consideration for the actual value of the stock. I've found that "old timers" tend to fall into this trap more often than younger investors. My guess is that their investing habits were formed long before modern electronics revolutionized all forms of investing. But then too, the increased popularity of trend-following technical analysis software is drawing many younger investors into this trap.

There are many reasons why the share price of a company declines—and those reasons may have absolutely nothing to do with the company itself. It might be a decline across the entire stock market, or it could be a drop in the specific industrial segment. It could be company-related, but still insignificant in the long-term prospects of the company. For instance, the company might report quarterly earnings a few cents lower than analysts had projected—that almost always triggers an immediate-but-short-lived sell-off of the stock by some institutional traders. It might be the recall of a product. The company might be the target of a lawsuit. Or a key executive who'd won acclaim for his innovations employed at the company might suddenly depart.

Any of these examples can lead investors to lose faith in the company's viability and sell off their shares in a fit of panic. Sometimes reacting to those news tidbits makes sense; often, however, the smarter move is to do nothing and then thoughtfully reevaluate the situation.

Investing requires patience. If the company's fundamentals and its prospects for future growth remain the same, the short-term price fluctuations of the stock are really irrelevant. You need to ignore the daily noise of the market and continue to focus on the fundamentals of the company.

Earlier I mentioned coming across investors who favor "cheap" stocks. The opposite can be a problem as well: too often, "bargains" scare novice investors. They would rather buy a stock on the way up than after it's taken a tumble.

So many investors love bargains at the supermarket, but prefer to pay a premium in the stock market. The lower the market, the less interested some investors are in investing. And the higher the market, the more driven they are to throw their money at it.

I have seen exactly this type of perverted logic hundreds of times.

Yes, it takes courage to invest when everyone else is selling, and resolve to sell when everyone else is buying. But that's how the best investors make their money in the market—by shedding their emotions and making their decisions based on facts, careful analysis, and the foresight of a long-term strategy.

5. BUYING OR SELLING ON EMOTION

Facts alone are wanted in life. Plant nothing else, and root out everything else. You can only form the minds of reasoning animals upon Facts: nothing else will ever be of any service to them. This is the principle on which I bring up my own children, and this is the principle on which I bring up these children. Stick to Facts, sir!

—*Charles Dickens*, Hard Times

We already discussed the ill-fated practice of making investment decisions based on emotions in the last chapter, but it bears repeating because falling prey to your emotions is the most common way investors sabotage their success.

Please, make your buying and selling decisions based on facts. What is the true value of the stock? Is the current price higher or lower than that value? If it's higher than the value you've given the stock, don't buy it just because the price is going up.

If the stock has dropped to lower than you paid, don't sell just because it's dropping. Sell because whatever caused you to buy the stock has changed.

By the way, my preferred investment vehicle, mutual funds, being baskets of stocks or bonds, do not have intrinsic value the way an individual stock does. Nevertheless, virtually all the other principles about when to buy and sell stocks apply to funds as well.

Instead of letting your emotions get the best of you, try to see corrections in the market as opportunities to buy at a bargain rather than to sell in a panic. That's how the most successful investors get a leg up on the market.

6. BEING TOO AGGRESSIVE

Often this mistake stems directly from Mistake #1, Chasing Performance. The investor sees some eye-popping mutual fund returns listed in the press or on a website and decides to pour an inappropriately large chunk of the family nest egg into those funds. Everything hums along nicely until pop, the market goes through one of its normal downturns, or worse, and suddenly the investor's plans for a relaxing retirement are gone with the wind.

Novice investors are the most likely to fall into this trap. They look at what they earn in a bank account, then look at annualized returns that are far higher for an aggressive stock fund, and it's, "Hey, I want some of that!"

As the hoary advice says, "Everything in moderation." Too much of just about anything can kill you.

There are two basic ways to be overly aggressive as an investor. First, you can be fully invested in stocks or stock mutual funds that move up or down faster than the overall market. When these higher-volatility investments do well, they do very well, and when they fall, they plunge.

The other way to be overly aggressive is by excessive trading. Again, we can point back to Mistake #1. You chase short term returns, jump into a hot fund until it falls, and then you quickly move to another chart-topper, never allowing a particular approach to fully ripen. This type of investor can have a terrific year or two, but this kind of aggressive investing will almost invariably burn him or her, badly.

The best investors buy stocks or funds that they can hold for a fairly long period of time. They don't buy stocks or funds based on a hot tip that they may want to trade later in the week or month.

But perhaps the biggest danger of being too aggressive is that it could cause you to bail out of your long-term investment plan and swing all the way over to Mistake #7 . . .

7. NOT BEING AGGRESSIVE ENOUGH

Of all the boneheaded errors examined in this chapter, this is the one I see the most.

The volatility of the market keeps many otherwise intelligent individuals—even young ones—from putting their money into the stock market. But if you want to have your money in the most lucrative long-term investment available to most investors, you almost certainly should have a significant portion of your assets invested in stocks or stock mutual funds.

Fear and greed move the stock market, with fear of loss being more dominant than fear of missing out on big gains. Or as a psychologist might say, the pain of loss is stronger than the possibility of pleasure. In the financial world, we see this expressed in many ways.

For a few years following every major market meltdown, whether it was the 1987 crash, the bursting of the tech bubble in 2000–2002, or the Great Recession of 2008–2009, people become understandably skittish about the stock market. They focus on recent volatility rather than long-term goals. And as a result, they skew towards the more stable investments, holding more cash than they should. But that approach may not get you to your goals.

Many factors need to be considered when constructing a good investment mix. Here are several you need to consider before you invest:

- Your general health
- Your genetics (how long did your parents live?)
- Will you really need to live off this money, or is it going to be passed on to your heirs?
- What will your sources of income be once you are fully retired?
- How much do you need to live comfortably?
- What do you want to splurge on? How important are those things to you?

The fact is, our friends in the medical field have made long-term investing more difficult, because they are constantly increasing the average life span of Americans. And the longer you live, the more money you will need to fund your retirement.

An estimated 100,000 people in America are centenarians. How many of those lucky citizens, when they turned seventy-five, were prepared to make their money last another quarter century?

Are you prepared to live to a hundred? If you are currently in your fifties or younger, that is a very reasonable target. A couple of major breakthroughs in heart disease and cancer will be wonderful for the health and longevity of all of us, but there is also the potential for a financial disaster that will whack millions of unprepared Americans.

On a regular basis, I come across retired or nearly retired people who decide to move all their money to overly conservative investments in order to preserve their capital.

Let's examine the foolishness of that approach. You are in your mid-sixties, and you've just retired. You have a decent retirement savings account that will help you finance your retirement. So you decide to take all of your money out of stock funds and invest it all in government bonds that pay 2 percent (or less).

If you're, say, sixty-five and you're in relatively good health, you could live another twenty or thirty years. During that period, inflation could double or even triple the cost of everything you buy. What seems like a lot of money today may not be enough to cover your expenses ten or twenty years from now.

That's why you need to maintain some stock market exposure with your investment program—so you can grow your retirement savings to keep up with, or better, ahead of inflation. Those government bonds may be "safe" in terms of volatility, but they are not likely to keep ahead of inflation, especially after-tax inflation. That's not safe—that's dangerous to your financial health. As the years go by, you'll find it increasingly difficult to pay your bills.

If you want to enjoy a fulfilling retirement, you almost certainly need to keep at least a portion of your savings in the stock market. While those investments may bounce around in the short-term, they are, based on history, likely to be the best investments to help you stay ahead of inflation over the long term.

Chapter 5

WHY DON'T YOU HAVE A PLAN?

Every Journey Needs a Destination,
Which Is Why You Need a Plan

If you don't know where you are going
you'll end up someplace else.
—*Yogi Berra*

Did you ever head out on a trip without a destination in mind? That may have happened a time or two in your youth, but as you get older and wiser, you recognize that things tend to work out better if you take the time to plan out where you want go, what you want to do, and how you want to get there.

A successful journey through life can benefit, as well, from advanced planning. The more you plan, the smoother things tend to go. Yet many intelligent people go through life without ever considering putting together a financial plan. They might have a savings account, a 401(k) plan at work, life insurance, and perhaps a few random investments. But they've set no meaningful objectives and made no specific plans to take the steps needed to meet those objectives.

Do you know where you want to be financially in ten years, twenty years, retirement? Do you know how you're going to pay for your children's education?

And the big question that applies to almost everyone: Do you know how much you'll need to fund a secure retirement?—and how much you'll need to save or invest to reach that level?

If you don't already have a financial plan hammered into place, now is a good time to start. Once you come up with a plan, everything else begins falling into place. You determine what you need to set aside each week, month, quarter, or year to meet your long-term goals, and you take whatever steps you need to get there. That might mean tightening the budget, downsizing your entertainment bill, becoming somewhat more aggressive with your investments, or even making a career change. But until you decide where you want to go, you can't begin to figure out how you're going to get there.

THE IMPORTANCE OF PLANNING

Planning is necessary, of course, in any worthwhile human enterprise; and while it might seem obvious that investing is one such example, I've seen too many investors attempt to go at it in fits and starts. Approaching the financial markets this way is foolish—even dangerous. Here's why:

- Without a plan that has clearly defined goals (preservation, appreciation, or income, for instance), you're more likely to be distracted by hot tips, big promises, and dubious deals that are not aligned with your lifetime goals. You may have too little insurance, or no savings regimen, or any of the other financial errors that fill this book. Spur of the moment investment ideas will have greater allure than carefully crafted long-term plans.
- You're more likely to deceive yourself about how much time you really have to accumulate the wealth you had hoped to accumulate.

HOW MUCH WILL YOU NEED?

There's no magic to preparing for a prosperous retirement. It's a matter of basic and simple math. Once you set your goal, a few calculations are all you need to figure what you ought to save each month.

It should be obvious that the sooner you begin, the easier it will be to reach your goal. Very few individuals begin a serious savings and investment program while in their 20s or 30s, but they could make their life a lot easier if they did.

As the tables below illustrate, the age at which you begin investing can make an incredible difference in the amount of money you'll need to set aside each month to fund your retirement.

The first table shows how much you would need to invest each month to reach $1 million by the age of sixty-five, depending on your age and average annual rate of return.

The other table shows what it takes to reach the inflation-adjusted equivalent of $1 million, based again on the age at which you begin and your rate of return.

Both tables should be helpful in determining your savings and investment objectives.

Table 1: Monthly contribution needed to reach $1 million by age 65

Starting age	25	35	45	55
Years to 65	40	30	20	10
Monthly contribution @ 5% return	$692	$1,255	$2,517	$6,614
Monthly contribution @ 7% return	$417	$880	$2,032	$6,038
Monthly contribution @ 9% return	$247	$612	$1,634	$5,482

Table 2: Monthly contribution needed to reach the inflation-adjusted equivalent of $1 million, based on a 3% annual inflation rate

Starting age	25	35	45	55
Years to 65	40	30	20	10
$1 million inflation-adjusted at 65	$3.26 million	$2.43 million	$1.81 million	$1.34 million
Monthly contribution @ 5% return	$2,256	$3,049	$4,555	$8,862
Monthly contribution @ 7% return	$1,359	$2,138	$3,677	$8,090
Monthly contribution @ 9% return	$805	$1,487	$2,973	$7,345

As would be obvious without any chart, you would need to save vastly more per month to reach $1 million at age sixty-five if you start at age fifty-five rather than age twenty-five. If you're twenty-five and earning a 7 percent average annual return, you could put away as little as $417 a month compared to $6,038 per month at age fifty-five if you're earning the same rate of return.

Adjusting for inflation, the young investors would need to crank it up a lot to reach the inflation-adjusted equivalent of $1 million at age sixty-five. For instance, with an average annual return of 7 percent, a twenty-five-year-old would need to put away $1,359 per month to reach the inflation-adjusted amount of $3.26 million compared to just $417 per month to reach exactly $1 million at age sixty-five.

Whatever your age, now that you can see what it would take to reach a million dollars (and a million dollars inflation-adjusted), you can look at your budget, determine a financial goal that makes sense to you, and start a systematic program putting away the amount you need to reach that goal.

Needless to say, however, retirement is probably not the only thing for which you'll need a sizable nest egg. If you don't already have a home, you may need to set up a savings or investment plan to come up with enough cash for a down payment. If you have children, you'll want to have a tax-sheltered (529) education fund to save for that very formidable outlay. These plans are the government's way of helping you save for college, and they are a good tool. If you are saving for a child's, or grandchild's, education you would be foolish not to take advantage of this option. You'll read more about the plans in the next section.

And don't forget insurance. While there is definitely such a thing as too much insurance, it does have its place. It's yet another component of a complete financial plan.

TYPES OF PROFESSIONAL FINANCIAL PLANS

Arguably the best approach to financial planning is to hire a professional planner with a solid reputation. Even though I'm a professional investment advisor, I use a financial *planner* to organize my financial life. (Investment advisors generally specialize in investments, while financial planners provide guidance with tax planning, estate planning, setting up trusts, etc.)

Financial plans often include dozens or sometimes even hundreds of pages of commentary to set you on your path. A comprehensive financial plan of that scope can cost several thousand dollars to prepare. With certain types of financial planners, when the plan is finished, your planner's job is done. That's right. Once they hand you the plan, the expectation is that you will use other financial professionals to help you with your investments and insurance. Your planner may be able to direct you to other financial professionals who can turn your plan into a reality.

The fact that they may hand you off to other professionals is not a bad thing. It can help ensure objectivity.

Other planners and financial advisors will offer to not only put together a plan for you, but will also provide the necessary investment products and management to implement the plan for you. Under those conditions, the cost of the financial plan itself is typically much lower—maybe a few hundred dollars—because the advisor is able to make money by enrolling you as a client and earning commissions on the sale of mutual funds, stocks, bonds, insurance products, annuities, and any other investment products she allocates for your portfolio. In fact, some advisors offer a free financial plan to any new clients as an incentive to attract new business.

As you might guess, I'm not a fan of that approach.

Many of the "free" or inexpensive plans are data driven. You put in the numbers and the analysis software spits out a plan with the budget requirements, contribution levels, and projected returns necessary for you to reach all of your financial objectives. The more costly, in-depth plans may also be computer-generated in part, but typically include some human analysis by the planner and some specific input unique to your personal situation.

Before you enlist a financial professional to prepare a plan for you, you should research the field of planners in your area, and interview the best candidates (either by phone or in person) to see which type of working relationship makes the most sense to you. If you already have a trusted accountant or investment advisor, he or she may be able to recommend a financial planner for you.

COMPONENTS OF A FINANCIAL PLAN

You don't have to go the professional planning route to get started on your financial plan. You can start the process by spending an evening or an afternoon putting together a plan on your own. It's not a difficult process. And once you've done it, you're no longer swinging in the dark at an unknown target. You'll have a goal and a purpose. You'll know where you want to be, when you want to be there, and what it will take to get you there.

A financial plan typically includes several key components:

- **A budget.** It's a lot easier to make a plan once you know exactly where all of your money is going. Whether you're on your own or share your life with a working spouse, figure out how much money you take home each month, how much you spend on necessities, how much you spend on non-necessities, how much you contribute to charities, and how much you sock away in savings or investments. As you get further into the planning process, you may find that you need to make some tough alterations in your budget to meet all of your long-term costs and objectives.
- **A goal.** Where do you want to be financially at age sixty-five (or earlier, or later)? Are there other costs besides retirement that require a substantial outlay, such as education costs, a new home, a second home, an exotic vacation? Set some timelines, add it all up, check out the two tables posted earlier in this chapter, and figure out what you would need to sock away each month. If you don't have the income to make that contribution each month, it's good to know that now. It means that you'll need to make adjustments—either in your goals, your budget, or your income (maybe you need to delay retirement). The sooner you have a plan, the sooner you begin to take the necessary steps to follow that plan.
- **Emergency fund.** The general rule of thumb is that you should try to put away enough money to cover any emergencies that may arise, or to cover your basic expenses in case you're laid up, or laid off, and unable to make a living for around six to twelve months. This money goes into an absolutely safe, liquid, and convenient spot, which typically means a savings account at a bank. It's probable you won't make much on that money, but this money is not part of your investment nest egg. It is, as it's commonly called, your rainy day fund.

- **Retirement funding.** What are you going to need in order to live comfortably after you retire? What does that mean adjusted for inflation? You may have no idea what your financial needs will be years from now when you retire. Just give it your best guess. The rule of thumb here, and it's a *very* rough guide, is that you can withdraw 4 percent of your nest egg each year after you stop working, and not outlive your money (assuming your nest egg is invested intelligently, usually something like a 60/40 mix of stocks and bonds). That means, if you have a million dollars saved up, you can take out around $40,000 each year, adjusted for inflation. Whatever your goal, write it down, check out the tables above, and make the calculation to see how much you'll need to invest each month, at your age, to reach that goal. Document it. Save it in your computer. Print it out, and make it your goal. Then follow up. Make it happen, or adjust as necessary. Read through your plan periodically to see if you're staying on track. Your financial prosperity depends on it.

- **College fund.** Here's another massive budget strangler. Three children, four years at a good college can run you between a quarter million and a half million dollars—and a great college would cost you even more. If you have children, higher education tuition could be a big part of your future costs. The only other option—unless your kids are either spectacular athletes or scholastic geniuses— is leaving them with a virtually insurmountable student loan debt before they've earned their first paycheck. So, if you want to help your children with their education, you need to set up a college savings plan. A Coverdell Education Savings Account (ESA) sometimes referred to as an "educational IRA," will allow you to save $2,000 per year, per child, per spouse. And the grandparents can also set up and contribute to a plan for your children, if they're so inclined. Investments in the account will grow, tax free, as long as the child uses the money for education by the age of thirty. Unfortunately, an ESA may still fall short of covering all of your children's college expenses for four years. Fortunately, you can also invest college funds in a tax-sheltered 529 plan. These are good vehicles for saving in advance for your children's education. The key for you is to find the money with which to fund them.

- **Insurance.** Savings and investments are just part of the package. You also need protection—for your assets, for your health, and for your family. A good, low-cost term life insurance policy that covers seven to ten times your income should provide sufficient income protection for your family. You'll also need insurance on your home and auto, as well as health insurance. Those are the basics. If you work for yourself, you should consider getting a disability policy to cover your expenses if you cannot work for some time. And as you're getting older, you should consider a long-term care insurance policy to cover the assisted-care and nursing home costs you might incur later in life. As with life insurance, the younger you are when you buy long-term care insurance, the cheaper the policy.

Unpleasant as it may seem now, getting an accurate fix on your future costs, and the challenges of preparing for those costs can only help. You're no longer flying blind.

You may even find that with a little structure, you can contribute all the money you need to fund your retirement and education accounts, as well as the cost of your insurance, without any difficulty. Congratulations! You have a future paved in gold. Maybe.

There's no question that for some, reaching your goals may require some serious belt tightening, more hours at work, or even a new career. Then again, it might just take a simple adjustment of your long-term objectives to a more realistic goal. Whatever you decide, it's good to have a plan. You'll never reach your destination if you don't know where you're going.

Chapter 6

ESTATE PLANNING:
WHAT ARE YOU WAITING FOR?

*I want to leave my children enough that they feel they
can do anything, but not so much that they do nothing.*
—*Warren Buffett*

If you love your family, you need an estate plan. An estate plan, by the way, is not exclusively for people who live on an estate. If you bought this book, the chances are very likely that you need one.

Not only can a good estate plan save your family many unpleasant days, months—even years—of dealing with contentious legal red tape, it can also provide some important benefits for you.

It could protect your assets and cut your taxes, both today and in the future for your heirs. It can dictate your medical care preferences when the situation arises, and it can give you the power to rule from the grave over the allocation of your assets for many years to come.

In short, an estate plan is a collection of legal documents designed to stipulate the administration and disposition of your estate, both after your death and/or if you're incapacitated.

Daunting as the estate planning process may seem, once you get the process started, it's really pretty routine. If you are married, you will have some important issues to discuss and reach agreement on with your spouse, but once you've gone through the key issues, your attorney will handle the documents and the details. Your job will be primarily scrawling your initials and your signature on a stack of documents.

In fact, you may already have started the estate planning process if you have completed a last will and testament. Your next step is to talk to an attorney to complete the other documents you'll need to finalize your estate plan.

It's hard to say what the greatest benefit of an estate plan may be because there are so many essential elements. The truth is, it all depends. If you have young children, the most important part of an estate plan may be the fact that it assigns a legal guardian of your choice to take over the care and upbringing of your children should you and your spouse not be around.

It might be the tax savings for you and your heirs, the ability to decide how to divvy up assets, or maybe the opportunity to decide how to handle your sensitive health care decisions when you're unable to do so for yourself. But the biggest advantage might well be the fact that an estate plan with the appropriate trust (or trusts) will allow your heirs to avoid one of the most frustrating, annoying, and time-consuming pursuits family members ever have to endure—probate court.

The point is, as difficult as it may be to address such sensitive issues as death and disability, an estate plan really is a good thing you need to set up for the sake of your loved ones.

COMPONENTS OF AN ESTATE PLAN

An estate plan typically contains several essential elements, including:

- **A will**. This is a contract that divvies up your money and possessions to the individuals of your choice after your death. But a will alone will not keep your estate out of probate court. To avoid the legal system and ensure that your estate is settled with a minimum of legal wrangling, you also need to set up a trust.

- **A trust**. There are several types of trusts that can be useful in estate planning. A trust is a legal document that gives you the ability to set aside assets to be given to your beneficiaries in a manner and a timetable of your choice. Trusts are also used to shelter assets from taxes. But the biggest benefit of a trust may be that it can help your heirs avoid probate court, allowing your assets to flow directly to your beneficiaries.

- **Power of attorney**. This agreement grants authority to another person to make legal decisions on your behalf in the event that you cannot.

- **Living will**. This is a set of instructions that stipulate the extent of medical measures that should be taken to keep you alive if you become unable to make those decisions on your own.

- **Health care proxy**. Also known as a health care power of attorney, this document appoints someone to make all health-care decisions for you in case you are incapable of making those decisions.

SETTLING DISPUTES

Setting up your estate can often bring up differences of opinion between you and your spouse on how the assets of your estate should be disbursed. For instance, maybe you've lost patience with one of your children and are tempted to leave that child out of your will. Your spouse may see things differently, and may perhaps point out that you would also be shunning that person's children—your grandchildren—by leaving that child out of your will.

Disagreements can come in many forms. I am not a lawyer, but clients do talk to me about anything connected with money, and frequently these disagreements are money issues. I've heard an amazing range of problems clients face when crafting estate plans.

You might disagree on how to divide your assets between your children and your favorite charities. You may differ on whether or not to leave children who are already financially secure the same amount as those who have a greater need. Issues regarding the grandchildren may also arise. Do you leave the same amount for a son or daughter who has one child as you do for another who has five?

Another sometimes contentious area regards the timing on the distribution of the money. Do you dole it out all at once or spread it out over time through a trust?

Chances are, you and your spouse have some differences of opinion that you're not even aware of. The sooner you can meet with an estate planner to get all of your ideas on the table, the sooner you can identify disputes and work toward a suitable resolution.

In most cases, a good advisor can walk you through your options and help you reach common ground. These can be very difficult discussions that may require compromise from both sides.

If compromise doesn't work, your estate planner may suggest splitting the estate into two parts. That way, the wife can decide how she wants to allocate her share, and the husband can decide separately how to allocate his part.

Your advisor may point out that trusts and wills can be amended later. But for now, you should reach a temporary agreement just to have a plan in place. If things change later—the black sheep of the family works his way back into your good graces, for instance—the will or trust can be changed to reflect your new outlook.

There are many factors to consider in setting up your estate. The sooner you meet with an estate expert, the sooner you can come to a decision on these important issues and begin putting your estate plan in place.

USING TRUSTS

Trusts can be an important part of your estate plan. There are different trusts that are used to address a wide range of issues. In certain circumstances, you may see the need for a trust that doles out money to your heirs in periodic payments. That can actually be a big benefit to the children since the money held in trust is usually sheltered from creditors. Better yet, if one of your children gets divorced, the part of the estate held in trust would not be part of the marital property, so it would all stay in the hands of your child, essentially sheltered from the ex-spouse.

The difference between a will and a trust is that a will is just a pile of papers that has no effect until you die—and even then it can be challenged in court. A trust can actually be a useful financial planning tool while you are still living, because it is much more resistant to legal challenges than a will, and it makes the distribution process almost automatic.

A trust can also speed up the probate process by eliminating the creditors' claims period that is required with a will. Setting up a revocable living trust can streamline the estate process and reduce the delays and conflicts in settling an estate.

Here are some of the more common trusts that may be useful for your estate plan:

- **Standby trust (Sometimes known as an ABC Trust)**. This legal document gives you the ability to assign someone else to manage your financial affairs in case you become incapable of doing it yourself.
- **Credit shelter trust**. This allows assets from one spouse to be used for the benefit of the surviving spouse, and then passed onto a beneficiary, such as a child or charity group.

- **Charitable remainder trust**. This gives you the opportunity to donate assets such as stocks or real estate to a charity and receive an immediate charitable deduction on your taxes, avoid capital gains taxes on the gains from those assets, and still continue receiving an income stream from those assets based on the market value.
- **Q-tip marital trust**. Similar to a credit shelter trust, this trust is designed to assure that children receive their inheritance even if their parents remarry. The trust would provide income and some principal from the estate to cover the spouse's living expenses, but most of the money would remain in the trust until the spouse's death, at which time the money would be passed on to the kids.

Like any legal document, creating a trust takes time, effort, and the use of an attorney, but the process is usually not as expensive as you might think. It generally costs about $1,500 to $5,000 to set up a trust, which is a small price to pay to help ensure that your beneficiaries receive the assets you intend in a smooth and timely fashion.

GOOD TO KNOW: THE DUTIES OF AN EXECUTOR

Now that you understand the benefits of an estate plan, it's also important to understand the flip side of an estate plan—what to expect if you happen to be named the executor of your spouse's or parent's estate.

So how is this "honor" bestowed upon you? The executor is typically named in the will of the person who has died. In most cases, the duties of executor are assigned to either the spouse or one of the older children. If you happen to have the unenviable honor of being the most responsible, most competent, most objective member of the family, there is a very good chance the duties of the executor will be assigned to you. If that happens, be prepared to spend a good part of your spare time going through documents, dealing with attorneys and investment advisors, and keeping the other heirs up-to-date on exactly how the process is going.

If no executor is named in the will, you and the other heirs can make the decision among yourselves, or if that fails, a judge can appoint an outside party as executor. In the case that the decedent has no spouse or children, a close relative may be assigned that duty.

As executor, you can earn a little extra money for driving the process and dealing with the other heirs—which can sometimes be a contentious process. Typically the stipend for the executor is around $25 an hour—somewhat more if it's handled by an outside party. The executor is paid from the proceeds of the estate.

If the deceased has done a great job of estate planning, your duties will be relatively easy. If not, you will suddenly be thrust into an unfamiliar and time-consuming situation that will require a level of patience, relationship skills, and estate expertise that you've probably never experienced before.

The most important function of an executor may be to keep the flow of information going in order to keep the other beneficiaries happy. The beneficiaries have a right to be informed on the progress of the estate process, and it's your job to do that. If you fail to keep them informed or to put in the time and effort you need to keep the process moving, the other beneficiaries can bring action to remove you for failure to administrate the estate in the proper fashion. And while that outcome would ease the burden on you, it really doesn't solve anything. Suddenly without you running the show, you could find yourself relying on another relative, just as inept—or more so— as you in executing the estate, and that could be even more frustrating than executing the estate yourself.

So, truth be told, if you're the one selected to be the executor, it would be in your best interest to do the best job you can to keep the process moving and your fellow-heirs happy. In the long run, that will lead to the best possible outcome for your family and you.

Now for the bad news: unless you can avoid probate, you will be dealing with a mountain of time-consuming responsibilities—the courts and the attorneys and all creditors and tax collectors, as well as the other heirs who will want to be constantly updated on the status of their inheritance.

If you ever find yourself in the position of executor, your key responsibilities will include staying in touch with all pertinent parties, getting an assessment of the value of all assets in the estate, safeguarding the estate, liquidating the assets as needed, notifying and paying creditors, participating in litigation, filing taxes, determining the amount of assets for distribution, making distributions, and closing the estate.

WHAT CAN GO WRONG?

The worst possible scenario is when the executor absconds with the money without paying creditors or beneficiaries. If you don't trust the executor, you can tell the court that you want that person bonded in the amount of the estate so that if the executor does head south with the money, the bonding will cover the distributions.

But even a competent and honest executor may face some snags along the way. If there is no will, the case may need to go through the courts to settle the estate, which could take months or years. Even if there is a will, there's a chance for that will to be challenged in court, which would hold up the distributions. The estate could also face legal challenges from creditors who dispute the decisions of the executor.

The bottom line is, as I mentioned in the beginning of this chapter, if you love your family, you need an estate plan. The more comprehensive the plan the less hassle your heirs will have to endure. No matter how thorough you are, there are still likely to be some difficulties and delays in settling the estate. But you can make the process much quicker and easier for your loved ones with a well-conceived estate plan.

Part 2

EYES WIDE OPEN

Chapter 7

WHY ARE YOU BUYING INTO
A BIG PROMISE?

A New Era of Con Artists, Hucksters, and Carnival Barkers

A man is his own easiest dupe,
for what he wishes to be true
he generally believes to be true.
—Demosthenes

"Step right up! Move closer! Are you going through hard times? Job loss got you down? You say your financial life isn't running at full speed? You've come to the right place, my friend. We've got just the remedy for what ails you—a remedy that's going to put *big* money in your pocket."

A big promise: that's how it all begins for the restless and vulnerable investor. If you're a fledgling investor, heeding the siren call of easy money—listening to a big promise—will probably be your first big mistake.

It's sad but true—when the economy sours, con artists and private placement hucksters flourish at the earnest investor's expense. They can smell your restlessness and are eager to help you make up

for the lost time of a sagging economy. But while unsavory charac-
ters flourish in hard times, they're con artists for all seasons, there
for the duration. They merely modify their pitch to suit changing
times. Their claim "we can make you big money," asserted during
hard times, simply transforms to claims like "we can make you bigger money" during a more robust economy.

What you as an investor must remember is never to buy into a big
promise. For that matter, never buy into *any* promise. Nobody can
predict the future. In the world of money, there are no sure things.
But you need to be particularly wary of big, sparkling promises. An
investment con artist knows he's unlikely to lure you with the mere
possibility of beating the Dow or the S&P 500 Index by a couple of
percentage points. (As you'll see later in the book, even that kind of
performance rarely comes easy.)

Sure, it would be helpful if the twenty-first century investment
con artist were as easy to spot as his nineteenth century and early
twentieth century predecessors. Like them, the latter day investment
con artist oozes the syrup of sincerity along with the assurance that
he (it's usually a he) can make you rich. Unlike the carnival barker
though, he's sophisticated. He won't be wearing a loud plaid jacket,
and no calliope music will be playing in the background. Worse, he
might even talk the talk of a Harvard MBA. For sure, he comes well
prepared with scripted reassurances and answers to every one of your
objections and is equipped with a full menu of dubious products and
deceptive practices designed to separate you from your money.

Periodically, the North American Securities Administrators Association (NASAA) releases a list of fraudulent financial products and
practices as identified by its Enforcement Section. Here are a few of
the top financial products and practices that have the potential to
trap unwary investors:

Financial Products
- Distressed real estate schemes
- Energy investments

- Gold and precious metal investments
- Promissory notes
- Securitized life settlement contracts
- Penny stocks

Financial Practices
- Affinity fraud
- Bogus or exaggerated credentials
- Mirror trading
- Private placements
- Securities and investment advice offered by unlicensed agents

By no means is this list comprehensive. For the latest threats, you can do an Internet search for "NASAA + top investor threats."

At this point, you might be wondering how these con artists can manage to talk you into putting your money into one of these dubious investments. The answer is simple—they are skilled and motivated. They know things you do not. They know the average person's strengths and weaknesses. In fact, once they get you involved in the conversation, the huckster is almost home. At that point, he need only prove why his big promise makes sense, and why you need to act immediately if you want in on the action. Then he goes for the close.

THE TIMESHARE SALES PITCH

Here's a little story from my own life. It's just one small example of how easy it can be to get swept up in the glow of an "opportunity."

While in Aruba in April 2012, my wife and I experienced pressure sales tactics at their best when we attended a presentation for a Caribbean timeshare program. Normally, we wouldn't carve out two hours from our vacation for this sort of thing, but that day was a rare gloomy day in that tropical paradise, and yes, we were enticed by the pile of free and substantial gifts promised to anyone who sat through the entire presentation. Also, I agreed to attend out of curiosity—these are pros at getting a point across—and it might be fun to see how they do what they do. Plus there was the fact that we were having a good time at the resort, so maybe this was something we could consider. I decided to go in with an open mind about time-shares, and, frankly, to see if anything I saw there could be applied to the book you are now holding.

On that last count, I was richly rewarded.

The young woman who was assigned to us was charming and friendly. For the first hour or so, she was our new best friend. She slowly and professionally built the case about the tremendous opportunity we were fortunate to have discovered. She showed us reprints about her company from major business magazines.

We were asked many questions, including "What's your ideal vacation?" and "How much do you usually spend?" Then she used our answers to make it seem like we absolutely had to agree that her company fulfilled our every holiday desire, and all for an amazing price. (Actually, it took her a very long time to talk about specific dollar requirements, but it sure seemed like we were going to get the deal of a lifetime—especially compared to all those *other* time-share programs out there. You know, the ones who played all kinds of shady games.)

She told us in great detail how the program worked, how easy it would be to make our plans, to stay where we want, when we want. And yes, she told us that unlike when we "rent" a hotel room and all that money goes down the drain, her program is "owner-ship." We would have "equity" in the timeshare we owned. In other words, she clearly implied this is a much better "investment" than a typical vacation.

For much of the time, she was jotting down numbers and lines and arrows to illustrate for us everything we needed to know. And then she began to write down all the special bonuses she could offer us, "If you sign up today. *And only today.*"

When we expressed the slightest uncertainty about the wonderfulness of the program, she brought over her manager, a man who in earlier times would have been called the "closer."

He turned up the pressure several notches. He made it seem like we were insulting him personally by not understanding the magnificence of the whole package laid out before us. He reiterated all the bonuses we would be turning down by not signing up right then. He told us, with a straight face and several times, that the value of what he was offering has never gone down, only up. And that, he said while looking directly into our eyes, would continue.

Even as I write this, it seems absurd. But I can tell you that despite my years of being in the world of finance and investments, his arguments sounded reasonable at the time. He spewed out apparent facts and figures, and both he and the young woman were low key. They never lost their friendly "I'm on your side" demeanor.

But we demurred, asking to think about it for a day or so. The dollar amount was nothing we could not afford, and we did in fact like much of what we saw. Nevertheless, we refused to sign right there, primarily because I have been preaching against this type of high-pressure tactic for years. Something just felt fishy.

Plus I also knew that timeshares could frequently be bought on the secondary market, directly from the original owner, for substantially less than from the originating firm.

We had asked to take with us all the notes that our female rep had written during the presentation. She looked concerned, and at one point said, well, I guess I could make a copy for you.

Turns out she couldn't. The manager refused to allow us to leave the room with any paper that contained the specifics of the offer.

Talk about a red flag!

Yet all around us, we saw couples signing up. Hell, at one point we were giving it serious consideration ourselves. But not giving us the details of the very product they wanted us to buy? It was at that point that I thought, "*KEN*, what the hell are *you* doing?"

About an hour after we left the sales room, the absurdity of the situation set in. How dare they ask us to commit to tens of thousands of dollars without giving us the specifics to study?

By the way, they never used the term timeshares. They insisted they are a real estate company offering a vacation program. But it was basically what most people who are not in their industry would call a timeshare.

As an investment, this did not make much sense. But it was a terrific learning experience. I felt what so many of you must feel when sitting down with someone who is selling insurance or annuities or virtually any sort of financial instrument. That is, it becomes terribly difficult for you to refute their "logic" when faced with a friendly face who clearly knows more than you about a particular investment.

You can avoid buying into a big promise if you stick to the fundamentals of investment decision-making—approach everything with a cool head, a clear plan, and some basic knowledge.

TAKE-AWAYS DESIGNED TO TAKE AWAY YOUR MONEY

As we saw in the session in Aruba, one of the contemporary con artist's most well-developed skills is his ability to employ the "take-away" close—or simply the *take-away*—the quintessential manipulation for winning your trust and sealing the deal. Let's look at some examples of the most frequently used take-aways:

The Limited Time Take-Away
- "We're only offering this deal during the next five days, after which we'll be registering all investor shares with the SEC."
- "After you leave here today (. . . or "After I hang up the phone"), this once-in-a-lifetime deal can no longer be made available to you."

The Available Shares Take-Away
- "We're only allocated 2,000 shares per investor. Can we lock you in for the maximum number of shares right now?"

The Right Fit Take-Away

- "Let me be frank. Some investors don't understand the idea of 'no risk, no reward,' and are afraid to venture into territory where *big* winners play. This special deal isn't for everyone."
- "I'll be honest." (Your guard should immediately go up anytime someone says that, or "Let me be frank." You should be thinking, *were you not honest up until now?*)
- We're not looking for people who have to take a second mortgage on their house to do this deal. Maybe this isn't your cup of tea after all." (Does it even bear saying that the con artist will accept your money from wherever you can unearth it?)

And when all else fails, the con artist will probably make one of the following plays for your hard-earned cash:

The Big Loss Take-Away

- "If you pass on this now, you'll be walking away from at least a couple of million bucks once the deal goes public in the next few months."
- "Think long and hard, can you really afford to let this one go?"

As I stressed in chapter 1, "you can't lose what you never had."

These are only a few of the verbal tricks unscrupulous investment sales people use to snag you. So don't bother to memorize them. Just remember the reliable maxim "if it sounds too good to be true, it probably is." Remember too, every big promise is accompanied by a trumped-up reason for urgency, a reason for you to wire funds or write a check *now*.

AVOIDING "PUMP-AND-DUMP" SCHEMES

"Pump-and-dump" refers to schemes by con artists to artificially inflate the price of a low-priced stock through various marketing tactics, and then selling those stocks at the inflated prices before they fall back down to earth—burning the investors who were gullible enough to put their money in those stocks.

Pump-and-dump has been around for years, but the methods keep changing as technology advances. The phone calls and newsletters of the past have given way to spam emails and website ads. But the intent remains the same—to promote the stock so that its value climbs quickly and then sell their shares at a profit. As they dump their shares, the stock price declines quickly, and the unsuspecting investors are left holding the bag.

How do you avoid pump-and-dump scams? In truth, it's not that hard. Here are two cardinal rules:

1. **Rule one: Don't buy a stock that's promoted in an email spam**. If the company has to resort to unsolicited emails or calls to promote its stock, you need to question the legitimacy of the company and the news release.
2. **Rule two: Don't buy a stock you've never heard of from a guy you've never heard of.** Deal with reputable advisors from a company you know. Pump-and-dump scammers often tie their offerings to hot topics in the news, such as high tech products or energy technology breakthroughs. Be wary of solicitors trying to hook you on investments tied to current affairs.

You should also be wary of any company that promotes its stock through unconventional channels. For instance, the SEC has busted companies that were promoting their stock through videos on YouTube.

What else should you watch out for? The SEC offers several tips to help investors avoid stock scams:

- **Consider the source**. When you see an offer on the Internet, assume it is a scam until you can prove through your own research that it is legitimate.
- **Find out where the stock trades**. Stocks traded in the Over-the-Counter Bulletin Board or the Pink Sheets are generally the most risky and most susceptible to manipulation.

- **Independently verify claims.** Don't take anyone's word about a particular stock. Be sure to get unbiased, objective advice.
- **Research the opportunity.** Always ask for—and carefully read—the prospectus or current financial statements and then check the SEC's EDGAR database (www.sec.gov) to see whether the investment is registered.
- **Be wary of high-pressure sales pitches.** Avoid promoters who pressure you to buy before you have a chance to investigate the stock. Don't fall for the line that you'll lose out on a "once-in-a-lifetime" chance to make big money if you don't act quickly.

Still not convinced, Dear Investor? Still holding out for the possibility that there's at least one big promise that represents your ship that's finally come in? Okay, fine. Let me make it easy for you. Unless you've lived on a deserted island without access to news reports these last several years, you need only remember two words to keep you out of harm's way: *Bernie Madoff.* Thousands of smart investors were unable to ignore "Uncle Bernie's" big promise of consistent, market-beating returns.

Sadly, I know one of them.

I have a distant relative who happily told me—around a year before the scandal broke—about all the money he had invested with Madoff. At the time, I never suspected it could be massive fraud. But I did urge my relative to please diversify because his returns were simply too good. "Anything that good is too far from the mainstream for it to continue. No one can keep doing that." Did my relative heed my advice? Nope. He kept the bulk of his nest egg with Madoff—and he lost millions.

My advice: Do absolutely no investing on the strength of a big promise. Remember, successful investing requires patience and discipline. Also, believe no investment salesman who taps into a need for urgency. A solid fund or the stock of a sound company will still be there if you take some time to think it over and do your due diligence.

Chapter 8

WHY DO YOU BELIEVE MARKETING HYPE?

It did what all ads are supposed to do:
create an anxiety relievable by purchase.
—David Foster Wallace

Hank and Martin (not their real names) run a successful and respected orthodontic practice in central New Jersey. They are friendly, obviously smart (other dentists send them their most difficult cases), and they have been clients of my money management firm for many years.

But for the first five years or so of our relationship, they regularly panicked when they received unsolicited direct mail packages that showed them why, with little room for uncertainty, the financial world was about to collapse. The packages, fortunately, offered them a path to financial salvation—for a hefty price.

The two dentists would forward the packages to me for comment. They seemed ready to assume that I would surely agree with the doom and gloom scenario so carefully and forcefully laid out in the text, and that I would therefore urge them to sell all their mutual funds and move to cash, or gold, or silver, or some other investment far afield from our middle-of-the-road mutual fund approach.

I never did agree to do that, of course, and after years of deflecting their panicky calls and emails, they have settled down and now follow the course our firm has carefully developed for them.

You almost certainly have seen some of those same direct mail pieces—yes, it's what most folks call junk mail. Millions arrive in mailboxes every year, and millions more are sent via email. Of course, the only reason those pieces keep flooding mailboxes and email inboxes is because they work. They bring in the profits for those who mail them.

Thousands of investors are indeed writing checks in response to these direct mail solicitations. If they weren't, the mailings would stop.

In this chapter, I want to inoculate you from the dangers of unsolicited financial direct mail advertising. I'm going to do it, in part, by jumping into the head of the typical guy who writes these pieces and dissect the process he uses. I think you'll find it fascinating, but more importantly, you will be better armed to fend off these powerful and emotional parries into your pocketbook.

YOUR "ROAD TO RICHES"

Here's what recently landed in my mailbox at home. Maybe you were lucky enough (ha!) to be on the same mailing list. Or maybe you read something similar after clicking on a website ad.

It was an oversized white envelope, a full eleven and a half inches wide instead of the normal nine and a half inches, with this message printed in large letters across the entire width of the envelope (quotation marks and underlines included):

> *"If you had listened to what I tried to tell you a month ago, you'd have made 1,065% in Lot78, Inc. I've just found a 90-cent stock that I believe could turn $10,000 into $245,500."*

That bold text, accompanied by what looked like a hand drawn arrow pointing back at the last sentence, was followed by another paragraph, flush left on the envelope and liberally highlighted in yellow marker:

"Lot78, Inc. made a fortune, <u>in under a month</u>, but now we're getting ready to do even better—and this time, I'd like you to join us in Tungsten Corp (TUNG)."
THIS AMAZING STORY IS INSIDE →

Inside was a sixteen-page letter folded into thirds. The first page was an explosion of **BOLD** fonts, yellow highlights, "hand drawn" felt tip marker lines and squiggles to draw your eye to certain phrases, and even something meant to look like it was torn out of another publication. Only after I'd scanned a full two-thirds of the way down the page was I finally greeted by the simple salutation "Dear Friend."

The letter overflowed with breathless prose and eye-grabbing graphics, all carefully designed to get the lucky recipients hot and happy about the opportunity that was about to unfold before their eyes in the ensuing fifteen pages.

A PEEK BEHIND THE CURTAIN

Why are investment solicitations like these so successful? Here's the secret the general population neither knows nor understands: there is a whole industry of professional direct mail copy writers and designers who specialize in getting you to start reading, keep reading, and finally, to send in your money.

These chameleon-like hired guns take on the persona of whichever financial genius they are working for at the moment. Today their message may be all doom and gloom to persuade you to buy gold. Next week, it might be all about economic recovery, so sign here to learn about some penny stocks that are poised to take advantage of this unique opportunity.

The direct mail pieces these professional copy writers turn out, working alongside world-class graphic designers, are honed and sharpened until *every single word* pushes you toward the final conclusion—the point where you say, "Yes! How can I pass this up? Send me my road map to incredible wealth! Here is my $495!"

In this industry, every aspect of each marketing piece is thoroughly tested—headlines, key phrases, offers, prices, and certainly the type of investment to push. Little if anything is left to chance. I know it well, because when I wrote my own investment newsletter, *Weber's Fund Advisor*, I was right in the thick of it. I got to know the leading lights in the copywriting world, and I personally hired a number of them.

The good ones—writer, designers, marketing consultants—command astronomical fees. They earn those fees because the packages they write and design tend to get checks and credit card numbers sent in by the thousands.

There are no accidents. Everything is tested, and re-tested, again and again. There is an art to writing good copy and designing eye-pulling graphics, but increasingly, the process has become driven by pure mathematics.

For example, these guys don't send the same piece to their entire list of a million or more prospects. No. Instead, they typically design and send several different pieces, all along the same theme but with two or three different headlines combined with two or three different sub-heads. The inside text might also be adjusted slightly. Changing a single word in a headline could mean a 10 percent uptick in the response rate—which can be a significant difference in the total response from a mailing of millions of pieces. All the responses are tabulated and the results analyzed microscopically.

These marketers are smart enough to realize that their success rate will be relatively small—usually less than one percent. But if they can hone their message well enough to bump up the response rate from say, 0.6 percent to 0.8 percent, that can add many thousands of dollars to *their* bottom line.

PUSHING YOUR BUTTONS

Let's take a second look at the message to see how cleverly this marketer is pushing your emotional buttons:

"If you had listened to what I tried to tell you a month ago, you'd have made 1,065% in Lot78, Inc. I've just found a 90-cent stock that I believe could turn $10,000 into $245,500."

Now, here's what's going on in the copy writer's head when he wrote:

"If you had listened . . . "

First, the lines are in quotes. That sends a signal that "this is between you and me." It's not, of course, but that's the feeling they want to instill.

The words themselves, "If you had listened . . . " are designed to inject a little guilt. Suppose your life, and especially your financial life, is not going so swimmingly. *Well, my friend, it must be your fault, because I sincerely tried to help you! I don't know why you didn't listen to me then. But don't fret, friend, keep reading . . .*

" . . . to what I tried to tell you a month ago . . . "

Yes, just a month ago. Don't you remember? I tried to help you out, friend. Surely you're not going to make the same mistake again!

" . . . you'd have made 1,065% in Lot78, Inc."

Dear Investor, in those few words we have classic direct mail hype in all its glory. Look what's going on here.

First, specifics get better results than generalities. That's why the writer does not say, "I recommended a stock that went up by a factor of ten!" Nor did he say the stock went up 1000 percent. No. Instead, we humans find it more believable to be told that the stock, something called Lot78, Inc., went up *exactly* 1,065 percent. That apparent precision, that extra 65 percentage points over 1000, heightens the credibility. Or so it seems.

Now what about the pitch itself? I don't recall any previous letter from this guy touting Lot78. Did he really plug that stock, and if he did, through what means? Was it on some list of one hundred stocks to buy? Maybe he picked the one that did the best and used it as the perfect example in his mass mailing. (I simply don't know, but that's not the point; it is difficult or impossible to verify what was done previously.)

And when, exactly, did he make that recommendation—before or after the stock started rising?

Did he then send out another memo to tell us to *sell* the stock at the peak before it crashed? I don't recall receiving that either. Or maybe he used his marketing savvy to push up the stock price, and, in classic pump-and-dump fashion, bought at the bottom and sold at the top, pocketing a massive return in the process. We'll never know for sure.

Dear Investor, please realize that the government does nothing to protect you from these questionable solicitations. Being that the sender of these pieces is not an investment advisor (and therefore not subject to SEC oversight), the First Amendment pretty much protects everyone's right to say what they want. As long as the marketers are not committing outright fraud or libel, no government agency is in the picture. *Buyer beware*, indeed.

What we do know, because it is a matter of public record, is that Lot78 jumped from under $3 to a peak of over $24 in the span of less than a month. But within two weeks after reaching its peak, the stock price plunged all the way back down to $3. Those investors gullible enough to have put $10,000 in the stock at the peak would have seen their $10,000 drop to about $1,250 in just two weeks.

Someone made money on the stock, but it probably wasn't the small individual investor.

Was there any reason to buy the stock aside from the hype built up around it? Maybe, maybe not. In my opinion, its spectacular run-up had nothing to do with the company's prospects or fundamentals. Its growth seemed to be fueled by hype.

Continuing through the opening paragraph, the marketer tells us:

"I've just found a 90-cent stock . . . "

Let's back up for a moment. A few decades ago, before direct marketing became a highly refined art form, investors studied research reports sent out by the major financial firms. Those white paper reports were staid affairs that laid out reasonable facts, pros and cons, about a suggested stock purchase. That's quite different from these current direct mail pieces.

For example, a Kidder Peabody report from, say, 1965 would never have said, "I've just found something." Those reports, and others from the old-line firms, were institutional in tone, not conversational.

"I've just found . . . " implies timeliness (it happened *just* now), and more importantly, it implies it is something others don't know about. *I found this.* It doesn't say, "Here are a few reasons why our research department believes this might be a prudent stock for you to consider." No, it says, "Hey guys, look what I found!"

" . . . a 90-cent stock . . . "

It's an unfortunate observation that many investors, especially those well into the Social Security demographic, think a low stock price is worth searching for. I think it's a ridiculous way to invest, but the copywriter knows a low price is a great hook for a certain gullible segment of the investing public. And, again, it's nice and specific. It's not just "here's a low-priced stock for you," it's, "here's a ninety-cent stock. You like that, right?"

He continues:

" . . . that I believe could turn $10,000 into $245,500."

Are you seeing a pattern yet? That stock is not simply going to soar. No, it's going to take your ten grand and "I believe" turn it into . . . hold onto your hats . . . specifically, exactly, $245,500!

Ta da!

Next, on the front of the envelope were these words:

"Lot78, Inc. made a fortune, *in under a month, but now we're getting ready to do even better—and this time, I'd like you to join us in* **Tungsten Corp (TUNG)." THIS AMAZING STORY IS INSIDE →**

In other words, you missed the last one, but here's another chance. For goodness sakes, open the envelope and read about the amazing story of Tungsten Corp. (TUNG).

In just a few words, the writer has managed to:

1. instill guilt in his readers for failing to act on his earlier tip,
2. present a new chance to make up for the opportunity they missed, and
3. lure them into reading further to learn the secrets behind this phenomenal opportunity.

In case you're wondering, I did a little checking on TUNG after I received the mailing. Not surprisingly, it didn't seem to have quite the same magic as Lot78. The mailing informed us that TUNG was trading at 90 cents a share, and was poised to turn your $10,000 investment into $245,500. But by the time I checked out TUNG's stock chart, it had already plunged to 60 cents a share. Your $10,000 would now be worth $6,667—a far cry from the $245,500 you were led to expect.

MORE HYPE IN THE MAIL

Investment marketing pieces come in many forms. Let's dissect another one I recently received—this time a "magalog" (a combination of magazine and catalog it's the name the direct mail industry uses for the glossy sales pieces they disguise as magazines).

This particular one was twenty-four pages long, and in keeping with the illusion that it might be a legitimate magazine, it even listed a date in the upper right corner of the cover page, "Summer, 2013."

The magalog—which was tagged as a "Special Alert"—was titled:

Money & Power Edition:
DIAMONDS ARE AN INVESTORS BEST FRIEND

(Yes, they left out the apostrophe in Investor's, but they're not aiming for sophistication.)

Also on the cover was the photo of a prominent money guru, known for his appearances on TV business programs, looking solemnly into the camera. In a box to the right are three bullet points:

- BMX is my #1 stock pick
- Currently trading at $.60 with a long-term potential of $18.90
- Near term target of $3.78

Once you open the magalog, there's a plethora of beautiful photographs, compelling charts, creative graphics, and sincere, from-the-heart copy carefully crafted to win your heart. ("But my proudest achievement," the author humbly gushes, "is the work I have done to reach out to Main Street investors . . . to show them how to be a fox in Wall Street's hen house.")

Pass me the Kleenex.

Incidentally, I just had to check out BMX to see how this guru's favorite pick was panning out. The only news I could find on BMX referred to Bellamont Exploration, LTD, and said the company merged with Storm Resources in January 2012. The final stock price quoted for BMX was dated March 27, 2012, and showed the stock at thirty-six cents, down from a high of seventy cents.

I can't explain the purpose or motivation of highlighting a stock that stopped trading more than a year earlier. But there was a reason. There are no accidents in these direct mail campaigns. There is a purpose to every headline, every chart, every picture, and every word of copy—and that purpose, Dear Investor, is to separate you from your money.

THE BEST YET?

Let me examine with you just one more of these "extraordinary" opportunities. This one showed up in my email inbox, and it may be the best one yet.

Titled **"Your opportunity to Join the InvestorPlace 5-Star Trader's Alliance,"** the email pitch letter came with a "savings voucher" worth $9,975—and this warning:

"Disappears in 7 Days . . . No Exceptions, please."

Beneath the headline was a picture of a check made out to "Your Name Here" in the amount of $9,975.

Wow, does that mean I could be almost $10,000 richer just by signing up for this special offer? Well, not really, but that's the impression the email gives you to draw you into the pitch. Once they've got you, they just keep piling it on. Below I've included some of the high points of the pitch letter, with my own observations inserted in parentheses and italics to help guide you through the mind of the marketer. Directly below the picture of the $9,975 check were these bold subheads:

Never Before Have I Been Willing to Surrender
So Much Valuable Trading Expertise —107
Years of It, In Fact—For Almost $10,000 OFF.

But Circumstances Demand It. Please Read This Extraordinary Announcement In Full As It Will NOT Be Repeated.

(It's not clear what those circumstances are, but since it will "NOT Be Repeated" maybe I should read this.)

Become a Member of the InvestorPlace 5-Star Trader's Alliance Redeem Your $9,975 Voucher Today!

Dear Fellow Investor, Remember my cryptic note on Saturday?

(Not really, but I'll give you the benefit of the doubt.)

I'd like to hand you a handsome reward for being so patient.

(Great . . . I didn't realize I was being patient, but you can hand me the 10Gs.)

First, I NEVER thought I'd have the opportunity to do this . . .

After all, I almost NEVER get to hand our most loyal readers a one-time voucher for almost $10,000 in savings. But this is a truly special moment.

(What a break! I must have been born under a lucky star to be one of the "most loyal readers" of something I've never heard of so that I can get something he "almost never" gets to hand out. This really is "a truly special moment.")

*As you know, the market is becoming
increasingly fickle, jittery and volatile . . .*

*The Fed is wielding more influence than ever . . .
America's place in the world economy is under the
microscope . . . and Wall Street is as jittery as a June bug.*

*(It never hurts to strike a little fear in the reader's mind. But actually,
the Fed always wields vast influence, America's place in the world economy is always under the microscope and Wall Street is always jittery.)*

But it's strange. <u>*While most investors are
finding themselves dangerously exposed to
'flash sell offs'*</u>*—***<u>behind the scenes, an inner
cadre is capitalizing on this anxiety.</u>**

*In fact, they're going 180 degrees the other way
and loading up on SIGNIFICANT PROFITS as the
2013 'summer of anxiety' kicks off in earnest.*

*(What do they know that nobody else does? And how can I get in on
the action?)*

*I've pinpointed the 5 specific advisories leading the
charge . . . Here's an incredible snapshot I'd like to share:*

MIND BLOWING SUCCESS!

*Your Windfall Had You Bet $5k Each on the Top
10 Winners for Each . . . So Far in 2013 . . .*

*(A table of "Top 10 Winnings" is displayed, followed by more
commentary):*

*This table shows combined GROSS
WINNINGS of $187,328 . . .*

(Gee, that's great. Not profits but "winnings" from my "bet" of $5k on
each of the "Top 10 Winners." But I'm wondering how many stocks were
in the original pool of picks that produced this "Top 10 Winners" list. Also
wondering how the Bottom 10 did? And what was the average of all their
picks? We'll never know.)

*Wow! How would you like to go shopping for
a brand spanking new Porsche 911 — with
plenty of extra cash to accessorize?*

(I want the convertible. I can already feel the wind blowing through
my hair. If I had hair.)

(The pitch continues for another five pages of bombastic
hyperbole—**"where realistic expectations and enormous profits
meet"**—before the brains behind the operation are finally revealed):

*You get immediate access to every insight . . . every
buy and sell trigger . . . and EVERY SINGLE PROFIT
OPPORTUNITY doled out by our most proven traders.*

*Best of all you'll be partnering with the **Who's Who
of America's foremost stock pickers and traders**
including a true pioneer of advanced options trading
systems for the past 40 years . . . a Harvard Business
School grad . . . a former portfolio manager and senior
investment strategist at a leading hedge fund . . . a
best-selling author and co-inventor on two Microsoft
patents . . . a wunderkind and Wall Street guru
who made her first million before turning 30.*

See what I mean? The absolute crème de la crème . . .

(Well, that seals it. Are you kidding me—an actual "Harvard Business School grad"! Where did they find a guy like that? Not to mention a "former" hedge fund manager, and an author. This must be "the absolute crème de la crème.")

As you read on, you learn that the 5-StarAlliance boasts "107 years of world-beating trading expertise, 5 explosive services rolled into one, and immediate access to 13 Special Reports."

When you click on the "Join Now" tab, you're taken to a separate website displaying a large savings certificate with these words:

Hurry! Savings disappear midnight tonight.
Your official $9,976 savings certificate to join
the 5-Star Trader's Alliance
Only $3,000 Today! (Reg. $12,975). –
You save a mighty 75%!

(So if I wait until after midnight, I'll have to pay the full $12,975. But if I buy now, that means I'm $9,975 richer and it only cost me $3,000. What a deal!)

Whew. It's exhausting having all those promises thrown in your face.

WHERE DO THEY ALL COME FROM?

How many of these mailings have you received over the years? If you've ever subscribed to any financial publication or even any news publication, there's a good chance you're on mailing lists that are routinely sold to marketers like these with a story to sell. Yes, another industry secret is that some publications make a very nice income by selling names of past and current subscribers to other marketers. In fact, some low-priced publications exist primarily to "harvest" names and addresses which are then sold for a tidy profit. The names of current subscribers cost more than expired (not dead!) subscribers.

Again, this type of junk mail is sent out by the millions to investors just like you because it works. That is, it works for the marketer, but probably not for you. You *may* find a worthwhile nugget of information in these mailings, but in my experience, the odds of that happening are less than winning a bet by placing a chip on a single roulette wheel number.

Neither approach—casino gambling or buying over-hyped publications—is a smart way to invest. And yet, otherwise intelligent, successful individuals—such as my two dentist friends, Hank and Martin—fall under the spell of the hype.

Here's what I tell them, and here is what I want you, Dear Investor, to remember . . .

The barrage of slick direct mail will never stop, so never let your guard down.

These direct mail pieces, every single one of them, are one-sided diatribes, with little regard for facts. Their *only* purpose is to get you, the reader, to send in your money, and they will use every technique imaginable to push the "fear and greed" buttons inside every investor's brain. The best way to keep them from pushing your buttons is to ignore them and discard them as soon as they arrive in the mail.

It's called junk mail for good reason.

MORE HYPE IN THE PRECIOUS METALS MARKET

There's never a bad time to buy gold, according to the ever-churning hype machine of the precious metals industry: Buy gold to fight inflation! Buy gold because China is cornering the market! Buy gold because they can't mine enough gold to keep up with demand! Buy gold as a hedge against our weakening currency or as protection against Middle East turmoil! Buy gold because some day the price is going up to $5,000 an ounce!

Gold dealers constantly tug on our emotions of fear and greed to persuade us to line their pockets with your hard-earned money. And indeed, gold and other precious metals have had their moments—driven, in part, by the hype of the precious metals dealers.

Even when gold was trading at $1,900 an ounce in September 2011, the gold bugs continued their push to persuade investors to buy before it runs up any further. Fear and greed—the perfect combination. In the ensuing two years, gold dropped 25 percent to around $1,400 an ounce. But there were no apologies from the gold bugs . . . just more hype. Buy now. Get in before hyperinflation hits. Buy before the dollar collapses. Buy before the Euro collapses. According to the gold bugs, there's always a good reason to buy more gold.

Here are some facts to consider about gold. The world is not running out of gold. In fact, gold is being used less and less for industrial applications (not to mention dental work). China has no interest in cornering the market. And if the world financial markets collapse into shambles, everything, including your gold, will decline in value.

You almost certainly don't need gold in your portfolio, but if it helps you sleep better at night, you may decide to use gold as insurance against some unforeseen world calamity. I counsel putting no more than 10 percent of your nest egg into gold. A prudent and easy way to do it, in my opinion, is via a pure no-load mutual fund specializing in gold and/or other precious metals. Do just a little research on the website of a major firm like Schwab, Fidelity, or Vanguard, and you'll find plenty of decent choices.

A SUCKER BORN EVERY MINUTE

Great opportunities in the investment market are not going to arrive via third-class mail in your mailbox. Nor will they pop up in your email inbox. And they're not going to make you millions of dollars overnight.

Great opportunities come from diligent research and shrewd investment management over many years. Those that do that kind of work are not, repeat *not*, sending out breathless marketing hype asking for your money.

Do yourself a favor next time another investment pitch lands in your mailbox. Do not waste your time reading it. They are garbage, pure and simple, and should be "filed" as such in the proper receptacle.

Part 3

STOCKS, BONDS, AND COMMON SENSE

Chapter 9

WHY DO YOU THINK
YOUR STOCK CAN'T FAIL?

The Pitfalls and Perils of Investing in Individual Stocks

> *Bear Stearns is fine. Don't take your money out of Bear.*
> *That's just being silly. Don't be silly.*
> *—Jim Cramer, March 11, 2008,*
> *three days before Bear Stearns collapsed*

If I had a nickel for every time someone told me about a hot new company, I'd have, well, a pile of nickels, but that's beside the point. Unless you are very wealthy, you cannot make the assumption that any stock, no matter how glamorous its story, no matter what scientific breakthrough it has developed, no matter how many bold face names sit on the Board of Directors, has a lock on sustained profitability.

In other words, if you think you've found a stock that just can't fail, you need to check the history books.

Have you ever heard of the United States Leather Company? It was a can't-miss blue chip in 1900—and one of the original twelve components of the Dow Index. What about American Cotton Oil?

Distilling & Cattle Feeding? Tennessee Coal and RR? They were all original members of the Dow in 1896, and they are all, now, blowing in the wind.

In fact, General Electric is the only member of the original Dow still intact. The rest have been broken up, acquired, or, in the case of United States Leather Company, dissolved without a trace.

While macroeconomic forces were responsible for bringing down Bear Stearns, disruptive technologies have had an even more powerful effect on decimating some of the most dominant players of American industry.

For example, in 1999, Eastman Kodak ruled the camera and film market; its stock was trading at $75 a share.

Now it's a penny stock.

Ironically, more photographs are being taken nowadays than ever in history, but who needs film when pixels do the job just about as well, and far more conveniently? And who needs printed pictures when you have a gloriously bright and sharp iPad screen? The "Kodak Moment" has passed.

Entire industries rise and fall as technologies change. Print is not dead yet, but newspapers and bookstores are being steadily erased by the digital revolution.

In fact, tastes and technologies in today's world seem to be changing as rapidly as Apple turns out new iPhones—literally. Consider the case of BlackBerry, the world's first handheld wireless phone. Known as the "CrackBerry" in its heyday because of its addictive allure, the BlackBerry was the crème de la crème of the mobile phone industry just a few years ago. The stock was trading at over $120 a share as recently as 2007. But by 2013, after the release of several iterations of the iPhone and the Androids, the BlackBerry was suddenly passé. In late 2013, after BlackBerry scuttled an earlier agreement to be acquired, its stock dropped to about $6 a share—a 95 percent decline from its 2007 high.

Taking a can't-miss attitude toward stocks is a can't-miss recipe for likely failure. Kodak and BlackBerry are two of many companies that have been impaled by evolution. Here are a few other notable examples:

MYSPACE

Even in today's fast-changing global landscape, it would be hard to find any company that could match the meteoric rise and fall of MySpace. Although MySpace was never a publicly traded stock, its history is well documented. Founded in 2003, MySpace quickly grew to become the six hundred pound gorilla of the social networking world (even before "social networking" was part of the common vernacular). By 2006, MySpace had surpassed Google as the most visited website in the United States with a hundred million unique visitors per month. By then, MySpace was owned by News Corp., which acquired it in 2005 for $580 million. Rupert Murdoch was, no doubt, gloating over his spoils in 2007 when some analysts were valuing MySpace as high as $65 billion.

But there was a new kid in the social media mix named Facebook that was adding hip new features and streamlined operating functions that young consumers loved. MySpace failed to adapt, failed to innovate, and failed to upgrade the slow, stale interface that its users were growing to disdain (and ultimately abandon). In 2008, Facebook overtook MySpace in unique visitors, and things have only gotten worse for MySpace ever since.

In 2011, just five years after it became America's favorite web destination and four years after those estimates that it was worth $65 billion, MySpace was sold by News Corp. for just $35 million. By then, the site's one-time web-leading visitor rank had fallen to about three hundred.

Can you say irrelevant? Adapt or die.

BLOCKBUSTER

In the mid-1980s, Sandy Cook took note of America's sudden fascination with movie videos and decided that it would be a good time to get in the rental video business. At the time, about a quarter of Americans who owned a TV also had a VCR—a sum that was expected to double in the next five years. But her first attempt to buy into the business was rebuffed when the owner of the local video chain backed out of the deal. Undeterred by the setback, Sandy's husband, David Cook studied the industry and the prospects for growth and decided to open the first Blockbuster video outlet in Dallas in 1985. Cook's cavernous inventory of more than six thousand titles—including multiple copies of the most popular releases—dwarfed the sparse selection of all of his competitors. A specialist in database technology, Cook instituted a barcode system to discourage theft and track customers, and he designed an intuitive layout for his spacious stores, displaying the video sleeves like best-sellers in a book store.

Not surprisingly, the Blockbuster concept took off quickly, cashing in on the growing tidal wave of home VCR users.

In the late 1980s, Wayne Huizenga, the former highly successful president and CEO of Waste Management Inc., saw the growing potential of the video rental business and bought controlling interest in the company. With his deep pockets and management expertise, Huizenga implemented a rapid expansion program, opening thousands of new stores across the country. With the firm's rapid growth paired with Huizenga's reputation for success, the stock became a darling of Wall Street in the early 1990s. But as Hollywood Video and other video chain upstarts entered the market, the stock began to lose its luster.

Just the same, expansion plans continued until the firm reached a peak of 9,000 stores in 2004. But with the emergence of Netflix and later Redbox, Blockbuster's fortunes and its stock price were fading to black. The firm was forced into bankruptcy in 2010. Blockbuster and its remaining 1,700 stores were bought out by Dish Network in

2011. By 2013, DISH had closed more than half of the remaining stores, with dozens more locations shutting their doors each month. In many respects, Blockbuster's demise mirrored that of Kodak. Both were dominant kingpins of changing industries, and neither were able—or willing—to react and adapt fast enough to avoid obsolescence.

But not all the can't-miss companies that fizzle in the market can blame disruptive technologies for their failures. Sometimes Wall Street simply overestimates the commercial appeal of cutting edge new companies and overpays for the stock.

JETBLUE

Wait! JetBlue? Isn't that a thriving company? Yes, but for the sake of this discussion it's good to look back at its history.

In 2002, JetBlue Airways distinguished itself as a wunderkind of the travel industry. With its low-priced fares, "Getaway" packages, leather seats, spacious leg room, TVs on every seat, and satellite radio, JetBlue's prospects, like its spanking new planes, were flying high. During a downturn in the travel industry right after 9/11, the company showed uncommon promise among US airlines by actually logging a profit. It did so within six months after it commenced operations—a very unusual coup for any start-up, let alone an airline.

Lucky you if you were among JetBlue's very first investors on April 12, 2002, the company's first day of trading. The Wall Street darling opened at $27 and was trading at $41.27 by mid-day. That's a gain of more than 50 percent in one day. You would have been in good company, too. Even billionaire hedge fund manager George Soros got in early for a substantial equity position.

Fast forward to 2008 and 2009, the years when the travel industry, like many others in the US, suffered a severe decline. JetBlue posted a loss of thirty-seven-cent per share in 2008, and although it recovered to earnings of twenty cents a share in 2009, thirty-one cents in 2010, twenty-eight cents in 2011, and forty cents in 2012, the company still hasn't achieved the lofty results investment experts had been predicting. In late 2013, eleven years after JetBlue soared over $40 a share on its IPO opening, the airline was hovering just above the tarmac at just $6 plus change per share.

Perhaps it's still possible that JetBlue will soar again, but in a volatile industry where many of the giants have already been forced into mergers, the odds of JetBlue stock ever reliving its glory days are about as thin as the air at thirty thousand feet.

IT'S A SURE THING THAT THERE IS NO SURE THING

There are no sure things in the stock market—no can't-miss opportunities. Whether it's a blue chip pillar of the Dow or the hottest new concept on the net, every stock is vulnerable to an unexpected bolt of lightning that mortally wounds the firm—or merely sends the stock price down by 30 percent, 50 percent, or more. The problem with unexpected news is that it is, well, unexpected, and if that sudden bit of news is bad news, you need to be sure it doesn't severely deflate your personal financial balloon.

Let me be clear: if and when you do come across an investment opportunity that makes your mouth water, I do not want to dissuade you from buying that stock. People do become wealthy buying the Apples, Microsofts, and Googles of the world before they zoom into the stratosphere. The odds are not great in your favor, but it does happen.

Before you jump into any apparent golden opportunity, be certain that you have done your own high-level due diligence. Do not rely on a tip from a friend, relative, TV talking head, direct mail solicitation, a phone call from a broker, or any other source. The money you put into that stock is your money, not theirs, and if the stock plummets, you feel the pain, not them.

Above all, always keep in mind that relying on one or two positions, no matter how promising, leaves you vulnerable to financial disaster. Stay diversified.

Chapter 10

WHY DO YOU CARE
WHAT THE MARKET DID TODAY?

I don't read economic forecasts. I don't read the funny papers.
—Warren Buffett

Are you one of those people who pore over the *Wall Street Journal* every morning? Do you find yourself tuning into CNBC to check the market throughout the day? Do you log onto Yahoo Finance to see what your favorite stock is up to? Or down to?

Why?

Unless you're in the investment business, you truly don't need to know how the market is doing every business day. As I have said again and again in this book, and countless times to clients, it's better to take a long-term view of all of your investments—or enlist the services of a respected Registered Investment Advisor to manage your money so you can go on with the rest of your life.

Too many investors have gotten hooked on the daily investment talk shows. It's information overkill. You don't need to clutter your brain with the hourly movements in the commodities markets, the precious metals markets, or the stock and bond markets. You don't need to be concerned with the daily analysis of these economic and market experts.

Every financial talk show seems to present the same maddening scenario. Only the specifics change. One guest says energy stocks are the way to go and another guest says food stocks. One says buy precious metals, and another says it's time to dump your gold. In the end, what have you learned? Only that the opinions of the experts always differ, and there is no obvious answer.

Even as an investment advisor, I have to admit, I once fell into the same needless pattern. As with many financial pros that are about my age, years ago Friday nights found me in front of the television watching the great Louis Rukeyser's "Wall Street Week." The program always began with Lou talking to three renowned stock market pros. And Lou would usually ask them for a short-term stock market forecast.

But after a few years I realized a pattern was developing. One guest would say the market was going up, another said the market was going down, and the third somehow managed to disagree with the first two!

In other words, it became apparent to me that the talking heads we see on financial programs are chosen for their ability to, well, talk. They need to look good and sound good. Rarely do any of the shows call out the bad calls.

My best advice: turn off the talking heads and spend your time doing something more productive—or just relax and enjoy life.

DAILY QUOTES

Perhaps you are one of those investors who buy a new stock or mutual fund and then spend the next few days tracking its performance to see how your pick is panning out. It's a natural tendency.

But do you really need to keep following it every day or every week or even every month?

You don't check the value of your home or car every day. Why should you bother checking your investment values every day? Take the same attitude with your stock and bond investments.

Of course, it's true that every one of your investments has a new price every business day. In fact, your stock investments can change prices by the minute—and your mutual funds change every day. But those are not *your* prices. Those are someone else's prices, someone who is selling today. Your prices are months or years down the road.

In fact, you should stay away from stocks or stock mutual funds entirely if you foresee needing that particular chunk of money within the coming three or four years. If your time horizon is shorter than three or four years you need to keep that money in relatively stable investments such as short-term bonds, bank CDs, or money market funds.

The problem is that following your portfolio too closely can motivate you to make some bad decisions if you get caught up in the moment. And since there are always plenty of bad news stories to shake your confidence, you are more likely to sell out of fear rather than sticking to your long-term plans.

So assume you've made a good decision when you bought the investment, and then sit back and give it a chance to grow. Look at the market through a telescope, not a microscope.

The late Benjamin Graham, known as the "Father of Securities Analysis," laid it out bluntly in his book, *The Intelligent Investor* (New York: HarperCollins, February 2006): "The investor with a portfolio of sound stocks should expect their prices to fluctuate and should neither be concerned by sizable declines nor become excited by sizable advances. He should always remember that market quotations are there for his convenience, either to be taken advantage of **or to be ignored**."

Right on, Benjamin.

I DON'T KNOW, YOU DON'T KNOW, THEY DON'T KNOW: FINANCIAL MARKETS AND THE MEDIA

If you happen to be one of the hundreds of thousands of investors addicted to market watching, I can understand how you got to that sorry state. The financial media never stops making all of us feel like we absolutely must know stuff . . . the right now stuff.

But how much credence should you put in the commentary of the experts on Wall Street and the talking heads of the financial media? Almost none. I have been watching the financial markets for decades and I have yet to find a single one with a perfectly functioning crystal ball.

In other words, they don't know with any certainty what the future holds.

Never have, never will.

But individually, each "expert" will spout fiercely held arguments for why the market will go up, down, or sideways. And if you didn't know better, you might even think they actually do know the future.

They don't. They can offer perfectly plausible reasons for why the market went up or down in the past—20/20 hindsight is rampant on Wall Street. But they can't tell you with any certainty what the market is going to do next. Not this year, not next year, not ever, and since the media (almost) never calls them on their misses, they continue to prognosticate.

The financial shows, like most television, are entertainment, nothing more. If you enjoy that form of entertainment, feel free to keep watching, but don't expect to glean any gems of insight that will help your long-term performance. What advice would you follow anyway? Every guest touts a different stock, a different sector, a different strategy, or a different outlook on the market. You'd be investing in circles if you really tried to follow the experts.

There are a lot of ways to spend your time that would be much more productive—like playing more rounds of golf or spending more time with the kids.

But it's not difficult to understand why so many investors think they need to be concerned about the daily bumps and grinds of the markets. It's because the media beats it into them.

DOWN TO TWO DECIMAL POINTS

Recently I was driving home on a Sunday afternoon with my radio tuned to a New York City all-news station. The hourly five-minute business report was on, and it wrapped up with the "news" that the Dow Jones Industrial Average closed up 4.23 points on Friday, and the Standard & Poor's 500 Index gained 1.55 points.

Who was this "news" aimed at? And what purpose did it serve?

At the time of the radio report, the stock market had been closed for almost two full days. Anyone who cared about whether the Dow gained or lost a few points surely knew it by then.

More importantly, giving that two-day-old news could easily intimidate new investors. They would think that those numbers are significant—after all, they were still being announced days after the fact, and they were given to *two decimal places.*

The neophyte investor might think, "Why else would that smart 'business' reporter mention those results on the news if they weren't significant? I guess I don't understand finance."

But the fact is, those numbers are *not* important. For everyone except over-caffeinated professional day-trader type investors, the daily close of the Dow is merely noise, a snapshot of a fleeting moment, not worthy of concern for any rational long-term investor.

Worse, the numbers are given as, well, numbers. What in the world does "up 4.23" points mean to *your* portfolio? Did the Dow do better because it was up more "points" than the S&P?

This has been a pet peeve of mine for years. The only numbers that should be announced on the news programs are *percent* changes. Anything else is nonsensical because it is presented without context. In this case, the Dow gained 0.04 percent while the S&P gained

0.2 percent. In both cases, the net result would be that most broadly diversified portfolios barely budged from the previous day.

The practice of announcing point gains is a remnant from the days before calculators. Today there is no reason for broadcasting the raw numbers (which have almost no relationship to your nest egg), instead of the far more useful *percentage* gain or loss.

TAKE BACK YOUR LIFE

When you understand the inevitable ups and downs of the market, you will realize that following your holdings on an hourly or daily basis and micromanaging your portfolio can do little more than heighten your anxiety. There's no evidence to suggest that all of your worries and efforts will enhance your returns.

The United States Declaration of Independence talks about "life, liberty, and the pursuit of happiness." There is no mention of investments. Instead of gluing yourself to the financial news and the stock tables, free yourself to enjoy life. There surely are other things in your life you can spend your time enjoying—your family, your friends, your hobbies, or your sports. Read a good book or watch a good movie. The market will continue to evolve without your daily involvement. The time to get involved in the market is when you plan to buy or sell. Otherwise, declare your independence from the stock market to focus on your life, liberty, and the pursuit of your happiness.

Chapter 11

WHAT MAKES YOU THINK
YOU CAN TIME THE MARKET?

We continue to make more money when snoring than when active.
—*Warren Buffett*

Buy low, sell high. Do that over and over, and before you know it you will be wildly wealthy.

If only . . .

If you invest in stocks or mutual funds, it's only natural that you want to try to "time" the market. After all, why wouldn't you want to buy and sell at the best possible price?

Unfortunately, that seemingly simple goal is extremely difficult, if not impossible to attain with any regularity. In my decades of studying the market and watching leading market professionals make predictions, I know of no one who has been able to consistently call market tops and market bottoms.

Market timing is difficult, in part, because so many are trying to do exactly the same thing you are. And when it comes to the stock market, it is literally impossible for everyone to be right. Don't forget, when you buy a stock you are, generally speaking, buying shares from someone who is equally certain this a good time to dump those shares.

On occasion, you might actually succeed. You might buy a stock or fund just as it starts moving up or sell an investment just as it starts to decline. But let's be clear: it would be folly to let an occasional success give you the impression you can accurately time the market on a regular basis. "There are two kinds of forecasters," according to famed economist John Kenneth Galbraith, "those who don't know and those who don't know they don't know."

The problem with trying to time or predict the market is that you are pitting your wits and expertise against the sharpest minds and the most sophisticated computer programs on Wall Street—and even they miss the mark on a regular basis.

If the best and brightest minds on Wall Street frequently get it wrong, how can you expect to time the market successfully with any consistency? Legendary investment manager Peter Lynch put it this way in his classic best-seller, *One Up on Wall Street* (New York: Simon & Schuster, April 2000):

> Thousands of experts study overbought indicators, oversold indicators, head-and-shoulder patterns, put-call ratios, the Fed's policy on money supply, foreign investment, the movement of the constellations through the heavens, and the moss on oak trees, and they can't predict markets with any useful consistency any more than the gizzard squeezers could tell the Roman emperors when the Huns would attack.

And as William Goldman once observed regarding the brightest minds of Hollywood, "Nobody knows anything." Yep, when it comes to market timing, it's pretty much the same thing on Wall Street. Lots of folks make lots of noise about what to buy and sell, and when to buy and sell, but no one, repeat, no one, knows a single thing with certainty. The best any of us can offer are educated guesses.

The difficulty of market timing is not just a matter of opinion. It can be quantified through a variety of market studies.

HERE'S THE MOST IMPORTANT STUDY YOU WILL EVER READ ABOUT INVESTOR BEHAVIOR

The study was conducted by Louis S. Harvey, the president of DALBAR, Inc., a Boston-based research firm. He had his researchers track the gap between the performance of the Standard & Poor's 500 (S&P) Index and the average return of all stock mutual fund investors in the United States over twenty years ending December 31, 2013.

His results showed that the difference between the *market's* performance and the average return of *individual investors* has been staggering:

> . . . the average investor in all U.S. stock funds earned 3.7% annually over the past 30 years—a period in which the S&P 500 stock index returned 11.1% annually. That means stock-fund investors underperformed the market by approximately 7.4 percentage points annually for three decades, according to Dalbar." ("Just How Dumb Are Investors" by Jazon Zweig, *The Wall Street Journal*, May 9, 2014).

Please let that sink in for a moment. You, or someone very much like you, and millions of others, gave up around 7.4 percent, on average, every year for the past two decades.

Dalbar has been conducting this study for many years now and the results have been consistent. A Forbes.com article ("Fund Investors Lag as S&P Nears All-Time High" by Tom Anderson) from March 2013, explains this sorry state of affairs this way (emphasis added) . . .

More than half of the gap in returns can be attributed to performance chasing and other bad investing habits, DALBAR
found. The message from the DALBAR's yearly analysis has
been consistent since its first study in 1994: "No matter what
the state of the mutual fund industry, boom or bust: *Investment results are more dependent on investor behavior than on
fund performance. Mutual fund investors who hold onto their
investments are more successful than those who time the market.*

Except that paragraph should end with the words, " . . . who try to
time the market."

No one that I know of can time the market successfully with any
consistency. Period.

And if you do try to time the market, I have been saying for years
that the worst thing that can happen is that you turn out to be right.
Why is that the worst thing?

Because then you think you can do it!

You can't, at least not consistently over the long term.

SEVEN PERCENT CAN BE HUGE

At first, it might not seem like a big deal, but here's what that difference means in dollar terms.

Over twenty years, a $10,000 investment that grows at an annu-
alized rate of 4 percent would become around $21,068—a gain of
$11,068.

That same $10,000 investment at an 11 percent rate over twenty
years becomes about $72,633—a gain of $62,633. That is, you would
end up with a net return more than *five and a half times* the return
of a 4 percent annual rate. And of course, a $10,000 investment is a
small nest egg. If your portfolio is a multiple—and I hope it's a large
multiple of $10,000—then the actual dollar figure becomes vastly
more significant.

THE PROBLEMS WITH TIMING

Why is market timing so difficult? Three primary factors tend to trip up market timing investors:

1. The future is unknowable.

As Yogi Berra once put it, "it's hard to make predictions—especially about the future." Meteorologists have been trying to perfect the science of predicting the weather for generations, and yet, with all their advanced software, satellites, and computer technology, they still make plenty of mistakes. "Sunny" afternoons are suddenly interrupted by afternoon showers. Countless carefully planned picnics have been ruined by the well-intentioned but misguided prognostications of the local meteorologists.

Stock and bond markets, like weather patterns, are buffeted by countless forces, seen and unseen. Fortunetellers, palm readers, and astrologers are likely to be as accurate with their market predictions as anyone else—and no better. In fact, according to Warren Buffett, "The only value of stock forecasters is to make fortune-tellers look good."

There are so many factors that go into the movements of the market, including and especially the most fickle force of all—human emotion—that consistently forecasting how the stock market might move in the midst of all those variables has proven to be beyond the ability of humans or computer programs.

Truth be told, investor sentiment is often an excellent *contrary* indicator of the market's direction.

When a majority of investors expect the market to go up, it seems to go down more often than not, and vice-versa. There is a certain logic behind that; when "everyone knows" the market is going up, all the fuel for an upward thrust, that is, fresh cash flowing into the markets, is already in play. And on the other side, when pessimism rules the day, the bulk of the scared money has already moved out of stocks so the decline loses steam.

Years ago, Peter Lynch offered an insightful perspective on the difficulty of predicting the market based on economic forces in *One Up on Wall Street* (New York: Simon & Schuster, April 2000):

> Since the stock market is in some way related to the general economy, one way that people try to outguess the market is to predict inflation and recessions, booms and busts, and the direction of interest rates. True, there is a wonderful correlation between interest rates and the stock market, but who can foretell interest rates with any bankable regularity? There are 60,000 economists in the U.S., many of them employed full-time trying to forecast recessions and interest rates, and if they could do it successfully twice in a row, they'd all be millionaires by now.
>
> They'd have retired to Bimini where they could drink rum and fish for marlin. But as far as I know, most of them are still gainfully employed, which ought to tell us something. As some perceptive person once said, if all the economists in the world were laid end to end, it wouldn't be a bad thing.

And as someone else once said, "If all the economists were laid end to end, they'd still be facing different directions."

2. Market timing requires multiple decisions.

It might be easier to invest successfully through market timing if you only had to make one decision. But market timing requires a series of decisions. It's pretty obvious, but many people don't get it. If you decide, "now's the time to sell my funds," you then are forcing yourself to make another key decision—"When do I get back in?" You have to be right *both* times, or you may miss out on a fortuitous move in the market.

But how do you decide when to buy back in? If you wait too long, you could miss out on the market's rebound, failing to take advantage of your initial smart (or lucky) decision to sell. And once the market rebounds, the cycle begins again. Will you be lucky enough to time your next sell decision correctly, or will you sell too late or too early? Will a headline in *The Wall Street Journal* or a talking head on CNBC who insists that storm clouds are gathering cause you to be on the wrong side of the next big move?

I've seen it again and again; smart people who manage to give themselves the *worst* of both worlds—they sell near the bottom and then buy in near the top. The Dalbar study simply confirms my lamentable observations.

Market timing involves an endless stream of decisions that typically rely on gut feelings and blind luck. Over time, no one can get it right consistently. So don't try.

3. Emotions get the best of us.

OK, let's make a leap of faith and say that you have found some technical system, algorithm, or crystal ball that does a fine job seeing into the future. There is still a big problem—you are a human being and you have emotions.

Predicting future movements in the stock market is difficult enough, but having the patience and fortitude to actually act on your foresight with steadfast resolve may be even more difficult. The emotions of fear and greed combine to derail almost all but the most resolute investors. I've seen it countless times—investors who passionately inform me they prefer aggressive investments, but then when the market tumbles and they read or hear the opinions of "experts" that the market will continue falling, they panic and sell near the bottom.

Emotions are nasty things when it comes to investments. And few of us reliably know how we will react to different market scenarios.

THE BEST TIME TO TIME THE MARKET IS NEVER

So by now you understand why you should not try to predict market movements. I want to make it clear, however, that there is a difference between timing the market and moving in and out of specific stocks, bonds, or mutual funds.

Each investment must be chosen for a reason, or a series of reasons. All financial professionals make mistakes and rotate their investments, so it's likely you will do the same. Just be sure that when you change from one stock to another or from one mutual fund to another, you have a clearly defined rationale for every buy and sell.

As an investment advisor, we buy and sell mutual funds for clients based on changing conditions. But we never make any move based on our prediction that the stock market is going up or down—because we know we cannot make that prediction with any certainty.

And neither can you, nor anyone else.

INVESTING CAN MAKE GENIUSES LOOK DUMB

You might think that massive brainpower would help investors beat the market. But a high IQ alone is no guarantee of investment success.

Warren Buffett had it right when he said, "Investing is not a game where the guy with the 160 IQ beats the guy with 130 IQ. What's needed is a sound intellectual framework for making decisions and the ability to keep emotions from corroding that framework."

The history of stock market investing is littered with the stories of "really, really smart" folks who did dumb things with their money. That's why I constantly counsel that investors take a middle-of-the-road approach to investments, one that stays on a dull, but prudent, highway to long-term goals.

WHEN WILL THEY EVER LEARN?

Here it is, Dear Investor. Here, in seven words, is a succinct distillation of why I decided to write this book. A headline in the November 27, 2013 issue of *Bloomberg Businessweek* summed up my eternal frustration with how millions of Americans handle their money:

"Record Highs Lure Investors Back to Stocks"

And the sub-head to that headline was this kicker: "Cash pours into equity mutual funds after five years of withdrawals."

Do you fully grasp what those headlines mean? They tell us that huge numbers of investors did exactly the opposite of what makes sense; instead of piling into the market when prices were cheap, they waited until the market was expensive before buying stock funds!

How expensive? As the article points out, their hesitation caused them to "miss out as the Standard & Poor's 500-stock index almost tripled from its March 2009 low."

Sure, the stock market may still provide those latecomers with solid returns, but they have tipped the odds against themselves.

Are you one of those hapless folks who buy only after everything looks rosy? Let me ask you this: If a shirt you want is on sale at 30 percent off, do you say, "Nah, I'll wait until it goes back to its full price?"

I will tell you, Dear Investor, that when the stock market is high, here at Weber Asset Management we become inundated with new money from clients who are suddenly enamored with the market. We also get an influx of new clients who sometimes become frustrated if the account opening process takes slightly longer than they expected.

But when the market is down, it's crickets around here. Chirp, chirp.

Few clients add to their accounts, and few new investors come on board as clients.

Everything is backwards. People throw money at us after the market has doubled or tripled, and stop adding when stock prices are low. I have seen this scenario play out over and over. No matter how much we try to educate clients, we can't seem to overcome the inevitable pull of human nature to buy high and sell low.

Maybe you, who have taken the time to read this book, will help break that pattern.

IF NOT TIMING, THEN WHAT?

A shrewd, patient investor who could control his or her emotions could soar high above the masses by simply taking advantage of this inevitable trend. If you feel you *must* do some market timing, then the best thing you can do is follow Buffett's dictum: "Be fearful when others are greedy and greedy when others are fearful."

Basically, that is all one needs to know about any variant of market timing. No other system, chart-analysis, or tea leaf reading will likely produce better results. Sitting there reading this, it sounds so logical and simple—buy when others sell. But the next time an economic crisis hits, as banks are failing and nations are teetering on economic collapse, will you have the guts to actually buy more stock funds? Or will you give in to your emotions and fall in with the herd? As famed investor Benjamin Graham (considered the father of "value investing") succinctly put it, "the intelligent investor is likely to need considerable willpower to keep from following the crowd."

Please, Dear Investor, be intelligent.

Chapter 12

IF NOT NOW, WHEN?

Getting Started in the Investment Market

*A study of economics usually reveals that
the best time to buy anything is last year.*
—Marty Allen

As I explained in the last chapter on market timing, neither you nor I nor any other person on earth knows what the market will do next. But we do know with absolute certainty what has happened in the past. And if we know today that you can buy a great mutual fund for perhaps 15 or 20 percent less than the price of a few weeks ago, well, that is an opportunity that won't come around often.

Grab it.

Sure, the price may go down further. But it can also shoot back up and you will feel foolish for missing the bargain that was at your fingertips.

As I said earlier, too many people let their emotions drive their investment decisions. *Fear* keeps us from investing when prices are low, and *greed* pushes us to jump in with both feet when prices are high. I've been preaching about this for decades, but humans act from emotions and then rationalize those actions as best they can.

Yet a rising market drives the investment herds to buy at an increasing rate. And the higher the market goes the more eagerly investors put their money into stocks.

On the flip side, if the dumbest reason to buy a stock is because it is going up, the dumbest reason to sell a mutual fund is because it is going down. And yet, the lower the market falls the faster the investing public wants to unload their funds.

What's their reason? I've heard it many times: "I don't want to watch it go down any further." Which I translate as, "I will lock in my losses and prevent myself from participating in the eventual upturn."

There is an old expression in the investment community: *The best time to invest was twenty years ago. The second best time is today.*

We will never have precise indicators about when to buy and sell. The best any of us can do is to follow a few common sense guidelines.

DON'T BE MARRIED TO A STOCK OR FUND

Many clients come to us with a poorly performing portfolio, telling us they would prefer to hold on to those positions until they return to the break-even point. That rationale, again, has more to do with emotion than logic. The dollars represented by those shares have no memory of your past history. The questions you must ask are: "From today forward, where is the best place for these dollars? Which stocks or funds, which bonds, which sectors are the best now?"

Sometimes investors have an emotional attachment to a security. Maybe they work at that company or worked there in the past. Maybe their father worked there. Or perhaps the shares were handed down from a beloved relative.

I'm all for warm and fuzzy human relationships, but sorry, they have no place in your investment life. A stock, bond, or mutual fund does not feel about you the way you feel about it! (I have to remember this advice when I think about my beloved New York Mets.)

When it comes to investments, you must take a hard-nosed, cold-blooded approach based on facts and figures, not emotions.

Just to be clear, I am all for upgrading your investments as new opportunities arise. By cutting some of your underwater stocks and funds, you can save on your tax bill. But please avoid the psychological blunder of fruitlessly waiting for your losers to return to your purchase price merely because you don't want to sustain a loss. You need a better reason than that for holding on.

THE AUTOMATED ALTERNATIVE TO MARKET TIMING: DOLLAR COST AVERAGING

There actually is an alternate strategy to market timing that helps tip the odds in your favor.

Dollar cost averaging entails nothing more than investing a set amount of money at regular intervals. As a result, when prices are high, you buy fewer shares. When prices fall, you buy more shares.

Over time, a mathematical quirk sets in, one that tilts the odds in your favor. Your average cost per share will be lower than the average price of the stock over the time you've been doing it. More on that in a moment.

You don't hear much about dollar cost averaging on the financial shows, do you? That's because once you fully recognize the effectiveness of this simple technique, you really don't have much use for "news." Markets go up, markets go down. The endless prattle about *why* they move this way or that is entertainment, nothing more. No one truly knows which of the thousands of gyrations in the economy are truly responsible for the movement in the markets today. And for sure, no one really knows where the market is going tomorrow.

But I do believe that if you purchase a fixed amount of a broadly diversified mutual fund on the first day of every quarter, over time you will have better returns than the talking heads on your favorite financial shows.

What's that? You don't have a favorite financial show? You don't even watch any financial shows? You're smarter than you realized.

HOW TO DOLLAR COST AVERAGE

You can set up a dollar cost averaging plan in a matter of minutes, and once you've set it up, there are no more decisions to make.

Start by deciding on a schedule, a contribution amount, and a target investment. For example, you might set up a checking account deduction plan that automatically withdraws $500 a month from your account each month or each quarter to invest in a particular stock or mutual fund. That's it—that's all you have to do. And then the mathematical magic begins.

The volatility of the market takes care of the rest. As mentioned above, the market's vacillations provide endless opportunities for you to automatically buy *more* shares when the market is down and *fewer* shares when stocks are up.

For instance, if you allocate an automatic investment of $100 per month in an index fund, when the market is high and your fund is trading at $10 per share, your $100 will buy ten shares. When the market is down and shares are trading at just $7.14, your $100 investment will buy fourteen shares.

As you can see, you would end up buying fewer shares when the market is high and more shares when the market is low— automatically. It takes the market timing and emotion entirely out of the equation.

WHEN TO DOLLAR COST AVERAGE

Many investors use dollar cost averaging not only to build their overall portfolio, but also to build a position in a single fund or stock. Speak to ten different investment professionals, however, and you will get ten different opinions about the best way to do that. Some suggest stretching your purchases out over as long as two years, especially when putting a large sum of cash to work in stocks. My own bias is towards a much shorter time frame.

My feeling is that since, over the long haul, the stock market goes up more often than it goes down, the odds favor getting in sooner rather than later.

Does this work to our advantage all the time? Of course not. But by doing a bit of dollar cost averaging we help ensure we don't put all the client's money into the market at what potentially might be a market peak.

So while there clearly is no absolute best way to dollar cost average, my strong suggestion is that you pick a time (first of every month, first of every quarter, whatever), pick a dollar amount, and then no matter what the market throws at you, stay with that schedule.

DOLLAR COST AVERAGING VERSUS TIMING THE MARKET

You may be wondering, if it's so simple, why doesn't everyone use dollar cost averaging? Because it is human nature to try to outsmart the market.

It takes us back to what I wrote about trying to time the market. People love to gamble. They spend billions of dollars every year at casinos even though it's common knowledge that the odds always favor the casinos. And too many in the investing public seek the thrill of the big hit. People think they can outsmart the market, but the landmines of miscalculation and human emotion invariably booby-trap their strategy.

So instead of trying to read tea leaves or esoteric charts to ascertain the direction of the stock market, make your life easy by instituting a good dollar cost averaging strategy, and then muster up the discipline to stick to it.

And by the way, when it comes time to sell, it can be smart to do some dollar cost averaging in reverse. That is, unless you need a chunk of money right away, plan on selling a fixed portion of what you need over a fixed schedule, i.e., once a month, or once a quarter.

Part 4

ARE YOU GETTING THE RIGHT ADVICE?

Chapter 13

THE PROBLEM WITH STOCKBROKERS

My stockbroker asked me something important today . . .
"paper or plastic?"
—Jay Leno

In my early days, when I was a much younger, snarkier investment advisor, I used to gleefully say that brokers are aptly named because that's what they make you—broker.

These days, of course, few people declare themselves to be a "stockbroker." Instead, their business card tells you that the person with whom you are speaking is a "Financial Advisor," an "Account Representative," a "Financial Consultant," or, increasingly commonly, "Vice President, Investments."

Right. Whatever. To my mind, if they work for a large financial firm and they in any way earn commissions off the products you buy from them, they are stockbrokers.

Some are good, some are bad, most are probably well-intentioned, but they all work under a business model that has a built-in conflict of interest.

More about that in a moment. First, a little look back.

Stockbrokers were plying their trade in the United States in 1792 when the New York Stock Exchange opened on Wall Street. They were a necessary component of the new form of capitalism taking root in the young, dynamic country. Without them, I readily concede, the economic engine that drove America to the top ranks of the world stage could have never appeared and flourished.

However, somewhere between then and now, their vaunted reputation became sullied.

"I do not regard a broker as a member of the human race," implored early nineteenth Century French playwright Honoré De Balzac. Irish writer Oscar Wilde wasn't much kinder: "With an evening coat and a white tie, anybody, even a *stockbroker*, can gain a reputation for being civilized."

Ouch.

While it may be unfair to paint an entire profession with the same brush, much of the scorn and skepticism directed at stockbrokers has been deserved. In fact, in my opinion, you should avoid letting any member of this endangered species come between you and your money.

That may be difficult advice for some of you to swallow. What about your Uncle Fred? He's been a well-respected local stockbroker for many years. In fact, he even gave you a good stock tip once during a friendly golf game. Now that you're about to retire, you've been seriously considering turning your 401(k) over to Uncle Fred to manage. Surely he wouldn't risk his family relationship by letting your account go off the rails, would he?

In due course we'll get to the subject of investing your money with stockbroker-friends or family. Right now though, it's crucial that you appreciate the most important reason why it's not in your best interest to invest with any stockbroker.

*It is my strong opinion that if a financial professional receives remuneration from transactions, you can never know for **certain** whether any particular recommendation has been made strictly with your best interests in mind.*

Put another way, traditional stockbrokers work on a transaction basis. What does that mean to you? It means the more trades made in your account, the more money the broker makes. *Whether or not those trades work out well for you is irrelevant to their bottom line.* All that matters are the transactions. Your broker is not motivated to find you great mutual funds or stocks or anything else that you can hold for the long-term—quite the opposite. They want to find you stocks they can convince you to buy today and sell tomorrow. The faster the "churn," the more they earn. Under the business model of some financial firms, they can't afford a client base of long-term buy-and-hold investors. That would put them out of business.

In fact, brokerage firms have little interest in how well their brokers perform for their clients. What gets brokerage firms excited is what they call "production"—which is their euphemism for transaction fees generated by their brokers.

An article in Research Magazine (April 2013) reported that a new training program at Merrill Lynch had resulted in a significant improvement in the production of new hires: "Last year, an unprecedented 68 percent of advisor trainees hit their production goals, resulting in record high revenue."

Exactly—*production goals.* That doesn't refer to the profits they *produce* for their clients. It's the revenue they *produce* for the brokerage firm.

My reaction to that article? So 68 percent hit their productions goals, eh? La di da. How does that help the individual investors? The fact is, all it means is that the brokers and the company earned more of *your* money.

Registered Investment Advisors (RIAs)—investment professionals who typically manage portfolios for their individual and institutional clients—(generally) don't have production goals. They must grow their business organically, with satisfied clients. Brokers—and, as always, that word is rarely used anymore—are revenue generators for their firm.

In order to achieve those higher production levels, the brokers have to come up with a convincing reason to persuade you to ramp up your volume of trades. Your broker's rationale for churning (a highly charged, pejorative term that I probably shouldn't use, but it makes the illustration easier to grasp) in your account may sound perfectly logical, and truly, he or she might be speaking from the heart.

He may say, "We bought this stock with a target price of $20. Now that it's reached that target, our analysts recommend you sell it and buy something else. Our analysts are now recommending that you buy XYZ, which they believe has exceptional short-term potential. "Or he might say, "When we bought this stock, we expected it to move up quickly to $20 a share. Instead, it doesn't seem to have any traction. So let's dump (or "trade up" or "move to" or "revolve into") this stock and put your money into something else our analysts are recommending that they believe will have better growth potential than the stock you are currently holding."

And then the charts and graphs and explanations will come out, and it will always look appealing.

But just because the rationale sounds logical doesn't mean the strategy is.

In the meantime, let's get back to Uncle Fred. Even if he were as altruistic as you'd like him to be, and even if he discounts his commissions for you, your personal relationship with him is fraught with potential problems.

That's because when it comes to your investments, you need a financial advisor whose feet you can hold to the fire. Or who can be fired. That's not so easy when the broker or advisor is a personal friend or relative. In my professional life, I tend to dissuade my closest friends and relatives from opening accounts with my firm. After all, just about the only thing I can guarantee in my business is that at some point the market will disappoint, and I don't want to have them feel awkward about expressing any concerns they might have.

This is not to say that your relationship should be contentious or distrustful. For sure, your goals should be reasonable and attainable. But more importantly, you need to be able to hold your financial advisor accountable. You need not be controlling. But you do need to take charge of the relationship.

You'll be less likely to maintain this kind of discipline with any variation of Uncle Fred. He was presented to you as the guy who won't let you down, the avuncular chap who passes on special tips to special people on the golf course. If you're one of Uncle Fred's special people, and if you think of him as your neighbor's relative who does you favors, you're unlikely to hold him accountable for anything. After all, it's he who's taking care of you, isn't it? Uncle Fred's in charge. And if there's anything for you to worry about, he'll be sure to call you.

Unfortunately, Uncle Fred may have other fish to fry. He might have stocks to "pump and dump" and commissions to rack up. He works under a branch manager, and the branch manager works under a district manager. They all likely have sales targets to hit, set by folks far removed from the head office. You, their client, may or may not be a priority for any of them, but don't bet your hard-earned money on it.

Lest you think this is exaggerated or cynical, consider the "confessions" of former stockbroker Joshua Brown in an interview with Bloomsbergbusinessweek.com ("Confessions of a Reformed Stockbroker" by Devon Leonard, February 28, 2012):

> In the late '90s, the thing to do was to become a broker . . . There were a bunch of people from my town, Merrick, NY . . . They graduated from college, and within a year they were making $200,000 or $300,000. They were knuckleheads in high school, now they were driving Porsches. It was definitely seductive . . .

And when the interviewer asks Brown what he thinks is wrong with the brokerage business (a business Brown eagerly abandoned), he confesses:

> The basic premise of a broker pitching a client is "I'm going to be able to consistently generate 20 percent returns a year or I'm going to consistently beat the market." They have no way to show any track record. They are managing hundreds of different accounts, each one is different. So I think it starts with a lie.

Brown further owns up to scenarios of canned pitches, and "advanced cold-calling skills." So the next time you think about Uncle Fred, think about the carefully constructed sales pitches, the push, the promises, and the Porsches. Think about the sheer numbers of clients he's looking to stuff into his client book. Then give some thought to Brown's characterization of a brokerage sales manager's admonition to his team of stockbrokers:

"Guys, we are not in the storage business. We are in the moving business. Keep the trades going and the money moving."

Being a seasoned financial consultant has nothing to do with offering tips on the golf course to selected investors like you. Uncle Fred may be a seasoned stockbroker merely because he makes two hundred phone calls a day. Or, if he's really good at what he does, he supervises a team of "junior stockbrokers" or "*frontiers*" who each make two hundred calls a day, and turn over the "hot leads" to him. His special gift is to persuade you that you're one in a million rather than the two hundredth call of the day.

A PROPENSITY FOR EXCESSIVE TRADING

Excessive trading is one of the most common complaints of the brokerage industry. Although the practice of churning is technically illegal, it's hard to prove. As I mentioned earlier, your broker will have numerous logical reasons for encouraging you to buy and sell stocks regularly. For instance, your broker would typically start the cycle with the advice to buy a stock *now* because his firm's Wall Street analysts think its price is in an ideal buying range. Then, the world turns, the economy flips and flops, politics intervenes (or merely seems to) and markets in general, and your stock in particular, reacts. So the broker persuades you to sell it and use the proceeds to buy yet another stock. It's an endless cycle of buying and selling that ultimately can earn your broker more in commissions than you reap for yourself in investment returns.

Even after years of pursuing an obvious pattern of churning, brokers are rarely held accountable for their actions. While there is an industry arithmetical standard called a "turnover ratio" against which your account can be measured, the brokerage house can summon several defenses. If you had given your broker discretionary control—the authority to trade stocks in your account without first consulting you—your broker can make the case that she was doing the best she could to earn a solid return for your account.

The brokerage house can also say your broker traded you out of particular stocks into cash, and then put you back in the same stocks because she was simply trying to protect you from a downturn in the market. Or it can argue she traded you out of those particular stocks and into other stocks because, through careful research, she discovered a better *opportunity* for you. The brokerage house might also cite "activity letters" it had continually sent you to inform you of the stepped-up trading in your account.

CONFLICTS OF INTEREST

Brokers may also be subject to conflicts of interest that can sabotage your investment portfolio. They are sometimes encouraged to push stocks in which their company has excess shares or with whom the investment firm has an investment banking relationship. Not only are they driven to persuade you to trade to pay the bills, they are often incentivized to compete with other brokers for extra bonuses and perks.

Be aware—a conflict of interest need not be blatantly obvious. It could be as simple as an inter-office contest for a trip to Hawaii. The point is, you just never know for sure.

How can you avoid the churning, conflicts of interest, high-pressure sales tactics, and other trading difficulties often associated with traditional stockbrokers?

Simple. Just don't use them. Find a registered investment advisor with whom you feel comfortable. He'll charge you a single management fee, typically a percentage of the assets under management, so that he is never tempted to trade your account needlessly. That way, he can focus on the long-term return of your portfolio.

With a single management fee, your advisor will be motivated by one objective—making your money grow. The more assets under management in your account, the greater your advisor's management fee. And conversely, if your account shrinks, so do her fees. Your interests and the advisor's interests are precisely aligned.

So it's no surprise that the transaction-based broker is becoming a dying breed. The advent of discount brokerage houses, the Internet and the growth of independent brokerages have seriously impaired the growth of these dinosaurs. Their share of the high net-worth investors dropped from 57 percent to 45 percent in just five years from 2007 to 2012 (according to an article posted on AdviserOne.com, March 2012), and their market share is expected to decline steadily in the years ahead.

To wrap up this chapter, take a look at this headline from an article from the *Guardian*, posted on its website (theGuardian.com) on November 25, 2013.

"Here's why Wall Street has a hard time being ethical"

The sub-head reads: "A new report finds 53% of financial services executives say that adhering to ethical standards inhibits career progression at their firm."

Got that? Please let that sink in: most executives in the business of investing other people's money admit that staying strictly ethical hurts *them*. The writer, a former trader goes on to say: "After a few years on Wall Street it was clear to me: you could make money by gaming anyone and everything."

Why in the world would you risk your nest egg to that kind of mindset?

As for your own dealings with the dinosaurs of the brokerage business, my most heartfelt advice to you, Dear Investor, can be summed up in two words: Steer clear.

Chapter 14

IS IT TIME TO REPLACE YOUR BROKER OR ADVISOR?

If you aren't fired with enthusiasm,
you will be fired with enthusiasm.
—Vince Lombardi

Job one for your financial advisor is to make you money. Everything else—the friendly smile, the market reports, the hand-holding during market storms—are all secondary to your actual bottom line.

If you've been with the same advisor for any length of time—whether a traditional stockbroker, a registered investment advisor, or a financial planner—and something just doesn't feel right, then it may be time to consider replacing your advisor.

It is important, of course, to have reasonable expectations for the rate of return your advisor is able to provide for you, and we reviewed expectations back in chapter 1. If the market has been in the dumps for a year or two, it would be unreasonable to expect positive returns for your stock-based investments. Your advisor cannot perform miracles. But if you find yourself trailing an appropriate benchmark (typically something like the Standard & Poor's 500 Stock Index for accounts that are all or almost all in stocks) by a significant margin year after year, then you are not getting your money's worth from your advisor.

Here are a few things you should do up front and then in the early days and weeks to help ensure a long and mutually profitable relationship:

- **Establish a clear understanding of the responsibility you're giving to the person who is handling investments on your behalf.** Does the broker or advisor have the ability to place trades in your account, or do you need to be called before any transaction takes place?

- **Most Registered Investment Advisors have you sign a *limited trading authorization* form.** This paper gives the advisor or broker the power to place orders, but, importantly, it typically does not allow for the money to be moved out of the account. The only exception should be to pay the advisor's fees. Any other withdrawal should be allowed to go to the "bank account of record" (i.e., your bank) or to your home address—and nowhere else.

- **Review your account statements regularly for accuracy and completeness.** Be sure all the transactions are on the statement and that they all make sense to you.

- **Ask questions about any action in your account that you don't understand.** While churning or embezzlement are rare, they do happen. Keep your eyes open. It's *your* money! Don't be afraid to ask questions. Trust me, there are no stupid questions.

- **At any time in the relationship, especially if dealing with a broker, report all unexplained or unauthorized transactions in your account.** If you are working with a stockbroker and he or she doesn't give you a satisfactory answer, go to his or her supervisor. If you still don't get a satisfactory answer, go to the company's compliance officer. If the firm can't answer your concerns satisfactorily, consider reporting the matter to your state's department of commerce—and perhaps to the US Securities and Exchange Commission. If you feel as though your broker has stolen money from your account, you could also go to the local police or sheriff's department or the county attorney. If they can't help you, they will likely refer you to the appropriate state agency. If the advisor is from another state, you should report your problem to the FBI or the US Postal Inspection Service.

As the relationship develops over time, here are red flags that indicate you may need to find another advisor:

- **Poor communication.** You need an advisor who communicates with you effectively. If he is constantly talking down to you or talking over your head about investments he is trying to sell you, that's bad. It's your advisor's job to simplify your life—not complicate it. You need an advisor who can ensure that you maintain a thorough understanding of what's happening in your investment account.
- **Inferior job of solving your operational problems.** Everything should run smoothly. Your advisor should work as your advocate; he or she should put *your* priorities first, not those of the large firm (Fidelity, Schwab, Merrill Lynch, etc.). You want to work with an advisor or investment firm that takes your issues seriously and makes an effort to solve your problems quickly and without repeated prodding from you.
- **Sells you investment products that are not in your best interest.** As I discussed in the last chapter, some brokers are more interested in generating commissions than they are in addressing your specific investment needs. If your broker is constantly trying to put you into products that don't seem

to align with your objectives—particularly high commission products such as annuities—that is a clear indication the advisor is more interested in her bottom line than she is in yours.

We discussed the practice of churning accounts in the last chapter. This practice of buying and selling securities at a rapid rate to generate commissions is one of the most common broker violations. If you believe your broker is churning your account, it's time to move your money elsewhere. In fact, depending on how serious it becomes, you might even want to report the broker to the firm's compliance officer or even to the Securities and Exchange Commission (SEC). Churning is a difficult charge to prove, but if you believe it is happening to you, at the very least, get rid of that broker and find another investment advisor.

There are six other specific violations that you also need to be aware of when dealing with brokers:

- **Unsuitability.** I'll discuss this in more detail in the next chapter, but brokers are expected to follow specific guidelines on the types of investments they sell to their clients. If your broker tries to put your money in investments that you consider to be too risky for you, such as penny stocks, options, futures, commodities, or other highly speculative investments, the broker may be violating the suitability rule.
- **Misrepresentation.** Stockbrokers, unlike most Registered Investment Advisors, are typically required to provide full disclosure regarding any investments he or she is trying to sell you. The broker cannot make false or misleading claims or guarantees about any investments. For instance, if a broker guarantees you that a stock or mutual fund will provide a specific return, that's misrepresentation. All stocks and mutual funds are speculative, and their prices are subject to the whims of the market, so their rate of return cannot be guaranteed. A broker may guarantee the rate of return of some

government bonds and insured certificates of deposit, but not the performance of a stock or mutual fund.

- **Unauthorized Trades.** Your broker is not allowed to make any trades in your account without your consent unless you have signed an agreement giving your broker discretionary control over your portfolio. If you notice on your account statement that the broker bought or sold any securities in your account without your consent, he or she is in violation of SEC regulations.

- **Overconcentration.** If your broker puts the majority of your assets into a single stock or even a single sector of stocks (biotech, precious metals, energy, etc.), that's considered over-concentration. Unless you have clearly agreed to something different, your broker generally has an obligation to help protect your assets by investing in stocks or mutual funds that represent a broader cross section of the market. Broad diversification will not prevent significant losses in a bear market, but it can prevent a severe loss if an individual stock or sector goes south. Whether the overconcentration was done intentionally by the broker or was merely unintentional negligence, it's still considered a violation.

- **Misappropriation.** In the rare instance when a broker takes money out of a client's account and spends it, flees the country with it, or uses it for other purposes, that is considered misappropriation. Misappropriation is a very serious violation, and can land the broker in prison for decades. Bernie Madoff essentially misappropriated his clients' money by running a Ponzi scheme in which he used money from new clients to make distributions to his existing clients. He also faced many other related charges, such as securities fraud, mail fraud, wire fraud, money laundering, and theft, but most of the charges revolved around misrepresentation and misappropriation.

- **Where Your Money Is Held Matters.** In the rare instances where outright fraud happens, if the broker works for a major brokerage firm, or your account is held at a major firm like Fidelity or Schwab, chances are you will be able to recoup most or all of your money, but not without some sleepless nights. On the other hand, if the broker or advisor works for an independent firm like, um, say, "Madoff Securities," and he has you make out your deposits to that company, God help you. In most cases the government will attempt to get some of your money back for you through clawback actions, but in many misappropriation cases, the victims lose most, if not all, of the money that they've invested.

If you believe that your advisor has violated any of the rules and guidelines discussed in this chapter, you should report the violation to the investment firm's compliance officer, and, depending on the seriousness of the violation, also to the SEC. Then immediately begin your search for a new advisor who will put your interests first. In the next chapter, I'll offer some advice on how to find a good advisor.

Life is too short, and your money too precious, to stick with a financial pro who disappoints.

Chapter 15

HOW TO FIND THE RIGHT ADVISOR

My job is to sell and buy, and not to reason why.
—Anonymous broker comment

Investors often view their advisors the same way voters view their elected officials. Americans have given Congress an approval rating as low as 10 percent, yet about 90 percent of Congressmen who run for re-election are voted back into office by their constituents.

The rationale seems to be, "Congress is terrible, except for my Congressman, who is pretty good."

Investors tend to look at the investment business the same way. In general, investors have a dim view of investment professionals in general, but they usually like their own investment professional

The fact is, there are good advisors and bad advisors and most investors are unable to tell the difference between the two. And while most investors give high ratings to their own advisor, very few can actually quantify that assessment.

Investors often tend to judge their advisors based on all the wrong things. They may be swayed by the advisor's effervescent personality, the firmness of his handshake, the richness of the wood paneling in his office, or the quality of his marketing material.

But none of those things should matter. The job of your advisor is, first and foremost, to make you money, prudently.

There are other factors that can also come into play: Do you get the service you want? Does your advisor answer your calls (or get back to you promptly)? Do you feel like the advisor sees you as more than just an account number? In the end, however, your advisor's primary job is to protect and grow your nest egg.

If you want an advisor who is most likely to keep your best interests at heart—and will be as motivated as possible to make your investments grow—I would highly recommend that you choose a Registered Investment Advisor rather than a traditional stockbroker.

As I stressed in chapter 14, the motives of the traditional broker are usually not aligned with yours. Your broker may be motivated to get you to buy and sell stocks as often as possible in order to generate transaction fees. Your investment performance is irrelevant to your broker's bottom line. What might really matter to your broker is the number of transactions he or she can persuade you to make in your account in order to boost his commission revenue.

One thing that's important to understand about many brokers is that a large chunk of the training they receive is related to sales—not investment management. Many brokers are innately strong sales people, and those who aren't receive the proper training to become very good at sales. The better their sales skills, the more successful they tend to be in terms of achieving a high income for themselves. But that does not necessarily translate into better investment performance for you.

You can eliminate that conflict of interest by choosing the right type of advisor to help you invest your money.

THE RIA ADVANTAGE

Fortunately, there are other options available beyond the traditional stockbroker—or worse, in my opinion, the insurance agent who "provides" mutual funds as part of their practice.

The best bet for you, I am convinced, is an advisor who specializes in managing money and whose interests are most closely aligned with yours.

Most Registered Investment Advisors (RIA) specialize in managing money, and they are usually compensated based on a percentage of assets under management rather than on transaction fees, so the number of trades in your account has no bearing on their fees.

As a result, it's in the RIAs best interest to see your account grow, because the more money you have in the account, the more the RIA will earn in fees. Their interests are aligned with yours, since you both benefit from a growing portfolio. They're not going to pressure you to make extra trades in your account. Quite the contrary. They are going to do everything they can to make sure your money is managed as effectively as possible.

RIAs are probably not going to try to sell you insurance or annuities, nor are they likely to offer you financial planning or estate planning. Most RIAs have a laser focus on their specific job—and that job is to manage the money you've entrusted to them.

A HIGHER STANDARD

Legally, RIAs are held to a higher professional standard than traditional stockbrokers. RIAs are expected to serve the "best interest of the client" with every security or investment product they buy on their clients' behalf. Putting the client's interests ahead of their own is a broad definition of the "fiduciary" standard. To my mind, that is the gold standard for investment professionals.

Stockbrokers also have standards—they are expected to meet a "suitability" standard—but that benchmark falls significantly short of the "best interest of the client" standard that RIAs must meet as the legal fiduciary for their clients.

For you as an investor, that distinction is important to grasp. The suitability standard simply means the broker is obliged to sell you investment securities or products that are *suitable* for your objectives, threshold for risk, means and age. For instance, a broker would violate that standard if he or she sold speculative stocks to a retired individual on a fixed income.

However, that suitability standard only goes so far. It doesn't require your broker to sell you the best possible securities or investment products—only products that are suitable for you. And that suitability standard can be broadly interpreted. It opens the door to allowing your broker to sell you anything that falls within your suitability range. It could be a mutual fund with a high load or a fund managed by the broker's own company that will earn the advisor a higher commission. It could be a stock the brokerage company has a position in that it wants to unload on the customers. And while the stock might technically be labeled as "suitable," it may not be in your best interest.

On the other hand, your RIA has a fiduciary responsibility—a legal obligation—to put your money in what he or she considers to be the best possible securities or products they can. They are also obligated to act in your best interest—not theirs.

In fact, from personal experience, I can tell you that at my firm we serve as the advocate for our clients in dealing with investment companies. If my client has an issue with Fidelity, for instance—regarding the cost or timing of a transaction or any other issues—we will act on behalf of the client to try to settle the issue favorably for the client. We are paid by our clients, and only by our clients, so our moral and fiduciary responsibility is to them, not to Fidelity, nor any other entity.

That won't always be the case with your broker, who may be swayed by conflicts of interest from within their firm. RIAs do not engage in business activities such as investment banking or underwriting, which can influence a brokerage firm to focus on pursuits outside their retail brokerage business and, potentially, to put their firm's best interests ahead of yours.

A LOOK AT FEES

Fees can also be an important consideration for investors, but don't get too hung up on fees. The bottom line is more important—your investment return *net*, after all fees. Most RIAs charge a management fee in the range of 1 to 2 percent of assets under management for their clients, although that can vary.

Most RIAs can tell you the returns they've earned for their clients in various types of investments. If you want a point of comparison when considering several investment advisors, the *net* return ought to be more important than the annual fee.

A LOOK AT RATES OF RETURN

That leads to another one of the biggest distinctions between brokers and RIAs. RIAs typically manage one or more model portfolios that can be tracked. Once an investment is tracked, a rate of return can be determined. But stockbrokers often don't manage a portfolio or set of portfolios. They simply buy and sell stocks for their clients—and the portfolios of each of their clients are almost always significantly different. Even if many of the stocks are the same from one client to the next, the transactions tend to be executed at different times and dates, and the percentage of each holding can vary dramatically from one investor to the next. That is why there's almost no way a broker can tell you the rate of return they have earned for their clients.

In fact, chances are your stockbroker couldn't even tell you what any specific return on investment has been. Calculating rates of return can be a very complex process, and often brokers have neither the expertise nor the interest to do it for you.

You can try to calculate it on your own, but it's not easy. With a bank account, you know exactly what you're earning because the bank will tell you, for instance, that you are earning a 2.5 percent annualized rate of return. Not so simple with an investment account.

The "internal rate of return" (IRR) is a method to provide an investor with an understanding of how well (or poorly) her account performed. To that end, IRR looks at all the cash flows in and out (every contribution, withdrawal, dividend, etc.) and says, "This is the money market equivalent rate you would have been earning in a bank account."

You can calculate the return over a year with a basic calculator only if, during that year, there was not a single transaction in the account. The moment there is any money movement in the account, an accurate calculation becomes far more complex. How complex? If you do an online search of "How to calculate IRR," you will find there is no universal agreement as to which exact formula to use. Here's one:

$$\text{NPV} = \sum_{n=0}^{N} \frac{C_n}{(1+r)^n} = 0$$

If that formula is over your head, join the crowd. The difficulty of calculating an accurate return is due to the ongoing action in your account—dividends, commissions, and transactions that constantly change the equation.

How else can you calculate a return? If you want to get a very rough estimate of how you're doing, there's another way to do it, but it's not going to give you a true return—just a general ballpark of how your investments are doing. And the more activity you've had in your account over the past year, the less accurate that calculation is likely to be.

Start with the total in your account at year-end and subtract the amount in your account from a year earlier. If you have $11,000 in your account now, and had $9,000 in your account a year ago, your total is $2,000. Then subtract all the money you've deposited in the account over the course of the year, and then add back any money you've withdrawn from the account and all the dividends you've received (unless the dividends went straight back into your account). If that total comes to $1,000, then your net gain is $1,000. Divide that $1,000 total by the $9,000 in your account a year ago, and your result would be 0.111—or 11.1 percent. Again, that's a very rough estimate of your actual return, but it normally should give you some idea of how your investment account is performing.

It's important to get some sense of your performance so that you can assess the job of your advisor. If, over a reasonable period you're not keeping pace with the market or an appropriate benchmark, then you may decide to move your money to another advisor.

Whether you use a stockbroker or an RIA, you're going to have good and not-so-good years. But if you have a year when the market is up 20 percent and you're up 2 percent, that's a big red flag. It indicates that your broker's approach is out of whack with standard investment practices, and it's a glaring sign that you should look elsewhere for your investment management.

CHOOSING A NEW ADVISOR

If you're looking for a new advisor, how do you sift through the nearly 400,000 brokers and RIAs in the US to find the advisor who is right for you?

Well, as is obvious by now, I think you should limit your search to Registered Investment Advisors.

You might begin your search by asking friends and relatives for referrals, but be sure that they can give you a valid reason for considering their advisor. If their reason is something to the effect of, "he's a great guy," that may not be a worthy referral. What you'd like to hear is that the advisor is responsive to their questions and needs, that the advisor took the time to learn about their objectives and threshold for risk before beginning the investment process, and that the advisor has produced a performance record that looks good.

Investment advisors sometimes offer free seminars to attract clients. Those seminars are often announced in a local newspaper. It may be worth your time to attend the seminars of two or three RIAs before you decide which one appeals to you based on their investment philosophy and their track record.

Once you've assembled a list of candidates, the next step is to schedule an appointment with that advisor to learn more about how he or she does business.

Track record, in my opinion, ought to be a paramount factor. But if the performance record of all of your candidates is similar, you can drill down further by asking a handful of questions that will help you determine if that advisor is a good match for you.

1. *How do you invest? What is your approach?* It can beneficial to learn the advisor's philosophy and investment approach to see if it makes sense to you.

2. *What types of investment products do you focus on in your investment process?* Again, the bottom line—the rate of return—is the most important factor to consider, but it's still worthwhile to learn the types of investments and the strategy the advisor uses to manage his clients' money.

3. *What types of investors do you work with the most?* Ideally, it would be good to find an advisor who has experience dealing with investors similar to you. Find out if the advisor works primarily with institutional clients, individuals, or a combination of the two. Are most of her individual clients retired or are they still working? Are her clients typically aggressive investors or conservative investors, or does she offer several portfolios with different management styles to appeal to both conservative and aggressive investors?

4. *If you're a conservative investor, you may be more concerned with how the portfolio does in a bear market—has the advisor been able*

to minimize the downside risk? If you're an aggressive investor, you might be more interested in how the portfolio does in a bull market. Aggressive portfolios tend to be more volatile than conservative portfolios, but they also often do much better in a bull market. The real question, however, is does the portfolio do well enough in a bull market to compensate for the volatility incurred, and does it deliver above-average long-term returns? If you're going to put yourself through the stress of a volatile portfolio, you should be rewarded with excellent long-term returns.

5. *How long have you been an advisor?* You may not need the most experienced advisor in the business, but you don't want a brand new advisor who is going to make all of his mistakes with your money. The ideal advisor would be one who, as an absolute minimum, has been in the business long enough to have managed money through a complete economic cycle—typically three to five years. Longer is much better; experience matters. By comparing the advisor's annual returns with the market averages through a complete economic cycle you can get a sense for her management style in both bull and bear markets.

6. *What type of service can I expect from you?* You may not have a preconceived notion of the type of service to expect, but it would be good to hear the advisor's approach to client service—and the rationale for that approach—to help you make a decision on whether that advisor would be appropriate for you.

7. *My spouse does not feel comfortable with investments. Do you make an effort to keep her in the loop? If something happens to me, will there be an easy transition for her?* Few investors think of these questions at the start of a relationship, but I can tell you from experience that when a life is in turmoil, a friendly and familiar person on the other end of the phone can be an invaluable and comforting resource.

There are really no "right" answers to any of these questions. What you're trying to do with the interview is get a sense for each advisor, how he or she conducts their business, and whether you would feel comfortable turning your money over to that advisor. In the end, you might find that one candidate stands out from the crowd, making it a very simple decision. But chances are you'll like more than one of the candidates. At that point, your decision will come down to which one has consistently delivered the best performance with the strategy that matches your objectives—and which one you feel most comfortable investing your money with.

EXPECTATIONS FOR YOUR NEW ADVISOR

A good advisor will ask you a series of questions to determine your investment objectives and your threshold for risk before investing any money on your behalf. If the advisor does not take the time to learn about you and your financial situation, move on immediately.

Your advisor should also lay out an investment plan he or she expects to follow to meet your objectives and adhere to your threshold for risk. And the advisor should set expectations for you. If you're a conservative investor, for instance, the advisor may caution you to lower your expectations regarding total return in your account. As I mentioned earlier, with a conservative portfolio, you're not likely to match the market when it's going up, but you should outperform the market when it's spiraling down. On the other hand, if you're an aggressive investor, your advisor should set your expectations regarding the volatility of the portfolio.

By the end of the discussion, your advisor should have a clear understanding of your investment profile, and you should have a clear understanding of the process and strategy the advisor will be using to manage your account.

There are many very capable RIAs out there who can do an excellent job of managing your money. It may take a little extra effort to find the perfect investment professional for you, but that effort should pay off in the long run with better investment performance, more peace of mind, and a larger nest egg to fund your life and your retirement.

Part 5

BEYOND THE STOCK MARKET

Chapter 16

WHY ARE YOU SPECULATING INSTEAD OF INVESTING?

There are two times in a man's life when he should not speculate:
when he can't afford it, and when he can.
—*Mark Twain*

Speculation: "Assumption of unusual business risk in hopes of obtaining commensurate gain" (*Merriam-Webster*).

If you ever want to get me angry, just tell me that you don't invest in the stock market because "it's a casino."

No, it's not at all a casino. In the casino, no matter how smart, disciplined or lucky you think you are, the house will always have an edge, and over the long run you will lose.

It's just the opposite on Wall Street. There, just about everyone wants you to win, and based on history, over the long run the odds turn strongly in your favor.

Nevertheless, there are those among us for whom the words "patience and discipline" are boring concepts. Those folks seek the thrill of the roll of the dice, the turn of the wheel, the flip of the cards. Tell them to have a time horizon of years, not weeks or days, and they smirk. They will think you are the sucker.

They are the speculators, and they give investing a bad name.

There are many ways to speculate in the investment market—options, futures, private placements, penny stocks, start-up businesses, turn-around stocks, and so on. By their very definition, speculative investments involve "unusual business risk" and, while *Merriam-Webster* points out that the risk is taken in hopes of obtaining commensurate gain, what it fails to mention is that, in my experience, the more likely result for the average speculator is commensurate loss.

Why do people choose to speculate? Boredom, impatience, greed, ignorance, and curiosity are all contributing factors. Or they simply fall prey to a carefully orchestrated sales pitch that lands them in penny stocks, restructured mortgage pools, currency options, or Florida swampland.

When you choose to speculate, you've made the decision to walk down the long, dark hall of high risk—vulnerable and alone. In most cases, there's no one to watch your back, no one to look out for your best interests. You're stepping into a smoky poker room full of sharks, and you've never played a hand. If you decide to try your hand at pork belly futures, for instance, you would be gambling against industry insiders who probably grew up on a farm, studied agriculture and commodities in college, and have done nothing but follow pork belly futures for their entire careers. What are your chances of outsmarting them?

Unless you have a particular expertise in a given area of the market, your chances of success as a speculator are very slim.

There are two important distinctions between investing and speculating. *Investors* attempt to achieve reasonable returns for their investment dollars over a long-term time frame of many years while most *speculators* are interested in a quick gain that hinges on a short-term movement in the markets. An investor buys stocks or mutual funds based on the underlying value and long-term potential of that investment, whereas (with some exceptions) a speculator has little or no interest in the underlying value of the investment or in its long-term potential, but is simply concerned with its odds of making a favorable short term move.

Let's take a look at some of the most common ways investors choose to speculate.

OPTIONS

I have spoken to many individuals who tell me that at some time in the past they "played around" with options and futures, but I don't know anyone who has done well over the long haul. Yet from 2004 to 2009, the volume of options trades done by individuals at Fidelity Investments increased by an astounding five-fold.

There are two basic kinds of options: a call and a put. A call option confers the right, but not the obligation, to buy the underlying asset at a specific strike price prior to expiration of the option, while the put option gives you the right to sell. If you win, by getting the price and timing right, your gains could range from a small profit to a substantial one. If you lose, by getting either the timing or price wrong, the most you can lose is the amount of money you originally put up, the amount known as the "premium." It's important to understand that a large percentage of options expire worthless at their expiration date.

One of the riskiest types of option trading is known as selling a "naked call," a transaction in which you would sell an options contract without hedging your bet by owning the underlying asset—which would protect you against unlimited losses in case of a significant and unexpected rise in the price of underlying security. With a naked call, the investor has no such hedge. Lots of folks have made lots of money with naked calls. Lots more, it seems to me, have lost more than they could have imagined.

Here's how these things work. Let's say you sell ten call contracts on a particular stock with a strike price of $10. Typically an option contract represents one hundred shares of a given stock, so ten options contracts would represent one thousand shares. In a typical scenario you might be able to collect $50 of premium per contract or $500 for all ten contracts when you sell the calls. If the stock price never reaches the strike price of $10, the options would expire worthless and you could keep your $500. But if the stock were to catch fire and run up in price to $20 a share—$10 beyond the strike price—you would, in essence, be required to buy one thousand shares of the stock at $20 in the market and sell them to the call buyer at $10 a share, suffering a quick loss of $10,000 (minus the $500 you received when you sold the contract).

Because of the high-risk factor of this investment strategy, some brokerage firms refuse to allow trades in naked options to someone who is new to options trading. You see? Even brokerage firms sometimes let logic stand before greed!

FUTURES

Simply put, a futures contract is an agreement between a buyer and seller on the purchase, sale, and delivery of a particular commodity at a specified price and future date. As with options, if you win, your gain could potentially be very substantial. But with futures, if you lose, you stand to lose *more than your initial investment.* (Which is also true of the sale of a *naked* option.)

Both the buyer and the seller must put up a small "good faith deposit" (called "initial margin"). The size of this deposit is determined by several factors, perhaps the most important of which is the recent volatility of the contract. Each day, the impact of the prior day's price change is settled up by the parties to the contract. Thus, if yesterday, the contract moved in the favor of the buyer by $2,000, the seller would be required to pay $2,000 to the buyer's account the next morning. This settlement process—called "variation margin" reduces the risk of default by the parties.

While futures contracts are traded on commodities futures exchanges for a particular delivery date—say March wheat or December gold—most contract holders close out their positions prior to contract expiration and roll them into a more distant expiration. Only those who want to take or make delivery of the commodity will carry the contract to expiration. In other words, you are not likely to see the purchaser of a futures contract take delivery of, say, 545 cattle, a half a ton of gold, or an 18-wheeler full of pork bellies. As a speculator, what you're aiming for is the cash profit of the transaction rather than physical delivery of the commodity. It should be noted that futures contracts on stock indices are not settled using a basket of stocks but rather by a final cash settlement based on the index level at expiration.

A long futures position is equivalent to being long a call and short a put on the commodity. Thus, the risk of a long futures position can be significant—remember what I said about short naked calls and puts.

Unlike the stock market, where you can use a margin loan to buy shares of a particular stock on a two-to-one basis, in the futures market, you can leverage your commodity at twenty-to-one because the "good faith deposit" is generally about 5 percent of the notional value of the contract! Because of the heavy leveraging potential, if you win, your gains could be wonderful. But if the market goes against you, your losses could be devastating. A small tick up or down in the price of a commodity can cost you thousands of dollars more than your original cash outlay. In reality, it must be said, few futures market participants utilize anywhere near twenty-to-one leverage.

WHO WINS?

At this point, you may be wondering, "If so many people lose in the options and futures markets, who benefits from playing the game?"

The broker who sells you your options and futures contracts makes money on the transactions, so he or she is happy to see you make those trades. And of course, the brokerage firm gets a slice as well.

But the big winners are the industry insiders who use your money to provide liquidity and insurance for their industry. For instance, let's say you decide to buy a futures contract to go long on gold—meaning that you are speculating that gold will increase in price. Betting against you is a hedger. A hedger in this particular case could be the owner of a gold mine who's interested in locking in the current price level of the gold he is producing. But because he's a professional, he knows that variables such as the value of the dollar and other currencies, as well as shifting economic conditions might affect the price of gold. So he sells a futures contract to go short on gold—meaning that he accounts for the fact that the price of gold could go down. By so doing, he bets against you. In this way, he'll also offset any loss his mine incurs on the price of gold (the price of his product) on the way down. Of course, if the price of gold were to rise, he would lose money on the futures contract, but that would be offset by the increased revenue he would get from selling the production of his mine.

The hedger has a lot of things going for him that you don't have: material resources, tax advantages, and history, among others. But his biggest advantage is greater access to information. I'm not saying that he can't be wrong and you can't be right. What I am saying is that the odds favor *him* being right more often than you. Whether the hedger is a gold mine owner betting against you on the price of gold, a farmer betting against you on the price of wheat, or a financial institution betting against you on stock options, the professional trader will almost always know a lot more about their areas of specialization than you do. You're a lone sheep in a herd of wolves. In fact, for the professionals, even a loss in the commodities market is considered to be simply a necessary cost of hedging their holdings. But for you, it's a straight-up loss.

Although it is true that the futures and options markets enjoy a semblance of orderly regulation through the US Commodity Futures Trading Commission (CFTC), the fact is, the CFTC is as much your friend as a casino owner in Las Vegas. You really do need to watch out for your own best interests because no one else will.

The futures market in the US began in the nineteenth century as a means of providing price certainty to farmers to ease their concern about the ultimate harvest price for their crops. Since that time, the principal virtue of the future markets is continually lauded as liquidity and as a way for hedgers to offset the price risk they incur. And the person on the other end of an options or futures transaction—most likely, the hedger—is a much more skilled and experienced player in the game than you could ever hope to be.

PRIVATE PLACEMENT

Few phrases in the financial world are as enticing as "get in on the ground floor." It's that sense of excitement that often pushes an investor to participate in a private placement. Sometimes getting in at the bottom results in fame, glory, and riches. Other times, the ceiling collapses and the early investor gets buried.

Private placements are a means of financing the growth and operation of start-up companies. Generally, private placements are funded by offering shares in the start-up company to a select group of people—as opposed to the stock of publicly traded companies, which can be bought or sold openly on a stock exchange.

Companies involved in private placements can do so without registering with the SEC under an exemption known as Regulation D under the Securities Act of 1933. The regulation was put in place for small young companies that would not be able to endure the high costs of going public.

Microsoft and Nike both began their corporate lives as private placements. Thousands of successful companies have started the same way, so private placements can become successful investments. But thousands of other companies that were launched through private placements fizzled and burned, leaving their initial shareholders with nothing but a worthless stock certificate to show for their investments.

How do private placements fit in with other speculative investments such as options and futures? They all share a common appeal: they cry out to investors to shake off their discipline and patience, and fly headlong into a "deal," all in the hope of realizing a big payday. But like options and futures, private placements are not for the faint of heart—and they are certainly not for investors with limited resources. Although the best private placements can pay off handsomely, they tend to be unproven, highly speculative businesses with low odds of success—especially the ones you're most likely to be invited or encouraged to invest in.

The most promising private placements are generally funded quickly by large banks, mutual funds, insurance companies, pension funds, and other industry insiders. But the more speculative "opportunities" are not snapped up quite so readily, leaving shares available for investors like you. In other words, the few private placements that do come your way would tend to have the greatest chance for failure.

So who does stand to benefit from a private placement deal? Obviously, the principal owners of the business that is being financed would benefit the most. They get to use OPM—other people's money—to finance the growth of their fledgling business. Another winner is, guess who? Yes, the broker who brought you to the table in the first place. And the investment company that put the private placement together stands to collect a healthy bounty. But what about you? With the prospect that you *might possibly* see an enhanced rate of return at some point in the distant future, you receive the dubious honor of being called an "angel investor." For that honor, you get to play a waiting game that could easily go on for five or ten years . . . or more—and possibly end with a complete loss of all your invested capital.

Before you buy into a private placement, you should also understand how difficult it will be for you to redeem your investment if you have a change of heart. With publicly traded stocks, if you make a mistake, you can bail out at any time by selling your shares on the stock exchange. But that's not the case with a private placement. There's no market for your private placement shares, so you may never be able to find a buyer for your stake. And the less success the company enjoys, the less likely it will be for you to ever find a buyer for your shares.

Are all private placement opportunities scams? Absolutely not, but that doesn't mean they're a suitable investment for you. Do you really have the time and expertise to sift through the financial information you will be provided? Will you really be able to assess the market for the product or service, along with its competition? Can you intelligently render a judgment about the management team and their likelihood of taking an idea from concept to profit?

And perhaps most importantly, do you have an adequate nest egg to afford to lose if things don't go well? With private placements, there's a very good chance you'll lose everything you invest, so please don't bet the farm.

As I've stressed throughout this book, the best approach to investing is to put your money in traditional investments with the idea of building a growing portfolio over the long term. Should that ever get too boring for you, please resist the urge to speculate. Buy a plane ticket to Las Vegas, take a roll of bills to the craps table, and try your luck there. You may lose your money just as quickly, but the adrenalin rush from the experience will be more pure, and the food and drinks are comp'd.

Better yet, don't do either.

Chapter 17

ARE HEDGE FUNDS RIGHT FOR YOU?

Test Question #1. In a given year, the Dow Jones Industrial Average rises 8 percent, the NASDAQ rises 7 percent, and the S&P 500 rises 9 percent. If, in that same period you manage a $29 billion hedge fund that loses 11 percent, how large a year-end bonus are you entitled to? (Round to the nearest $10 million.)

I found that joke on the Internet. It's funny, except it's also not funny.

Do you know what a hedge fund is? Most people don't—even if they think they do. If you're in the dark about these esoteric investment vehicles, consider yourself lucky. I hope you stay that way.

But if you insist, I'll shed some light on hedge funds with a quick overview. Hedge funds are similar to mutual funds but with some key differences. First, they are typically set up as limited partnerships. As such, they are not offered to the general public, and they don't, generally speaking, have to submit to SEC oversight. That allows them to use investing techniques which may be far more aggressive than your standard mutual fund. They might, for example, use options, futures and other "hedging" techniques as they seek outsized returns.

Some hedge funds swing for the fences; others use their special magic to try and deliver a positive return regardless of how the market does. Some reap big rewards for their investors; others blow up on the launch pad. Their strategies and investments of choice vary widely, but they all are limited to "accredited investors"—individuals who can meet fairly stringent income or wealth requirements. And that's a good thing, given the spotty returns that hedge funds have offered the past few years. But regardless of their investment style or track record, there is one overriding reason why I will never put any of my money into a hedge fund . . .

2 AND 20

What does that mean? Many of the major hedge funds charge a 2 percent annualized management fee. It's a permanent fee, charged regardless of how your investment fares.

Then—and this is the kicker—during the calendar quarters when they make a profit, they also take 20 percent (or more) *of your profits.*

Your profits. If there *are* profits.

As a result, Dear Investor, you could end up with a very paltry return while the hedge fund managers become obscenely wealthy. For instance, Steven A. Cohen, of SAC Capital Advisors made $1.4 billion in 2012 despite the fact that the investments of his hedge fund fell short of the market's returns for that year. And instead of the customary management fee of 20 percent of profits, Cohen charges 50 percent. Not a bad business—if I lose your money, you still owe me 2 percent of your investment, and if I make money, I get half of all your profits!

(On November 4, 2013, SAC pleaded guilty to fraud charges involving insider trading and agreed to pay $1.2 billion in fines and close its investment advisory business. According to "The Impact of

Settlement on SAC Capital and Cohen" by Peter J. Henning in *The New York Times*, the plea agreement allowed Cohen to continue to manage his personal fortune, estimated at about $9 billion.)

But Cohen is not the only hedge fund manager who has cashed in on mediocre performance at the expense of his clients. Ray Dalio, whose Bridgewater Associates also lagged the market indexes, consoled himself with $1.7 billion in take-home pay in 2012.

All told, the top twenty-five hedge fund managers earned an aggregate $14.14 billion in 2012, according to *The New York Times* ("Hedge Fund Titans Pay Stretching to Ten Figures" by Julie Creswell, April 15, 2013). That averages out to $565.6 million for each of the top twenty-five.

If the performance of hedge funds was decidedly and consistently superior to other investment options, such as good old no-load mutual funds, perhaps the exorbitant fees could be justified. But Cohen and Dalio are not the only ones delivering sub-par performance.

In fact, according to *The Times*, the majority of hedge funds have failed to beat the market for four consecutive years (through 2012).

Which begs the question . . .

WHY BOTHER?

With their lethal combination of high fees and spotty returns, what is it about hedge funds that attract thousands of smart, wealthy investors?

First, in most cases smart folks run the hedge funds, folks with glittering pedigrees from the best colleges and the sharpest financial firms. Some are math geniuses, some are physics majors from MIT, some are computer whizzes, and yes, some are literally rocket scientists.

Second, they all have a great story to tell. That story might be strictly about the brilliant minds running the shop, or it might be about how they have discovered a new technique or algorithm or research capability to do things better than the other smart guys.

Third, and this can't be denied: hedge funds—like high-end sports cars—are sexy.

A Maserati is sexy. Buy one and you are announcing your presence to the world. Sure, on the Long Island Expressway it can't go any faster than a Chevy Impala, but the Maserati snorts and growls, figuratively and maybe literally, in a way the Impala can't. Plain old mutual funds are Chevrolets.

Hedge funds, like Maseratis, hold within them the thrill of the hunt.

But guess what. Sometimes, as shown above, that patina of implied danger is well deserved. You probably don't want to take your wife or young kids out in a low-slung Lamborghini and zip around the hairpin turns of the highest peaks in the Rocky Mountains, and I strongly suggest you don't entrust your family's financial future to hedge funds either.

The reason I say that is straightforward: too many of the hot shot hedge funds have crashed and burned. Or simply skidded, or hit too many potholes. Why would you want to take that risk?

LONG TERM CAPITAL'S COLLAPSE

I can't have this discussion without bringing up the tragic story of Long Term Capital Management. It is the perfect representation of what can go wrong with hedge funds, and why you can't blindly follow "smart" people.

Long Term Capital Management began in 1993 with renowned Salomon Brothers bond trader John Meriwether at the helm. That got people's attention. Then they brought on Myron S. Scholes and Robert C. Merton to be on the Board of Directors. Do you recognize those names? Those two fellows shared the 1997 Nobel Memorial Prize in Economic Sciences for a "new method to determine the value of derivatives." Cool, eh? Who wouldn't want to be part of that club? And sure enough, the fund started with just over $1 billion in initial assets and focused on bond trading.

Well, to get to the end point, in 1998 Long Term Capital Management (LTCM) nearly brought down the global financial system.

They used sophisticated "arbitrage" strategies. I'm no expert, but it seems the fund had to leverage itself highly to make money. At its height in 1998, it had a debt-to-equity ratio of over twenty-five to one. Estimates were that the fund held or controlled positions that in total may have been as high as $1 trillion; at the time, an amount that size would have equaled roughly 5 percent of the total global fixed-income market.

Then a financial crisis hit Russia and a cascade of problems hit LTCM. It soon became clear that the fund was in danger of defaulting on its massive loans. But because of the fund's size, problems for LTCM were poised to become problems for the entire world.

In September 1998, LTCM, with its roster of the best and brightest, was bailed out with the cooperation of its creditors, and with the help of the Federal Reserve. That's what it took to avoid a market meltdown.

So much for the best and the brightest.

BUT SURELY THERE MUST BE ONE GOOD REASON FOR HEDGE FUNDS

It's the obvious one; people tell me they use hedge funds to, yes, "hedge their bets." That is, they seek an investment that is "non-correlated" to the biggest part of their nest egg; they want an investment that zigs when, for example, the US stock market zags.

Some hedge funds do offer that particular enticement. Many are specifically designed to move up or stay flat when the stock market falls. But are hedge funds, with their questionable fees and often dubious performance, the best approach to hedging your bet?

My response to that question is, and has been for many years, this: if you want to hedge your bets, *bet less.* It ain't that complicated.

By simply taking a chunk of your nest egg and moving it from higher risk investments to lower risk investments, you can achieve, more or less, what hedge funds offer without the attendant high fees and risks.

"HEDGE FUNDS ARE FOR SUCKERS"

That's not my opinion; that was the headline of the cover story by Sheela Kolhatkar for the July 11, 2013 issue of *Bloomberg Businessweek*.

The sub-head read: "Once seen as a ticket to obscene wealth, hedge funds have hit the skids. Why the industry's glory days may be gone for good."

That prediction may or may not turn out to be true, but I do know that every hedge fund, past, present, and future provides their prospective investors with a compelling story about why they are different from the other hedge funds. The problem, as always, is that neither you nor I have a way to figure out which story will lead to consistent profits.

And to drive home the point about hedge fund performance—that same *Businessweek* article contained a chart with the heading "Whiz Kids Lag the Market." It pointed out that hedges have not performed well over the longer term. "Over eight of the last ten years, simple market-pegged index funds have posted superior returns" compared to the HFRX Global Hedge Fund Index.

The bottom line, as I see it, is that some lucky souls (other than the hedge fund managers) will reap healthy profits, but many other investors will indeed become suckers, and they will help make some rich people even richer. It's your decision.

In my opinion, sticking to low-cost, no-load mutual funds from a respected, low-cost provider is a far more sensible approach than paying exorbitant fees to super-wealthy managers for questionable returns.

Chapter 18

ARE YOU BLINDED BY TAXES?

Don't Let the Tail Wag the Dog

If you are truly serious about preparing your child for the future,
don't teach him to subtract—teach him to deduct.
—Fran Lebowitz

Which is more, five or four?

Dumb question, right? Not really. Let me explain.

Without fail, after a good bull market run, I hear from a handful of clients who are upset because they were "hit" with a big tax bill on the capital gains we reaped for them. A few of these hapless investors even quit the stock market and moved completely into municipal bonds—just to reduce or avoid paying capital gains taxes.

There is a problem with that, which I'll come back to in a moment

I have been in the highest tax bracket for a long time (and for that I consider myself lucky and grateful, because it means I can provide a good life for my family and myself). I have found that people I meet, therefore, often assume that I invest heavily in things like municipal bonds or tax-efficient index funds. I do invest in those instruments, but they comprise only a small part of my portfolio. Over the long haul, I have done better by seeking out the strongest, smartest investments possible. And for most people I speak to, that would also be the best strategy.

So again, which is better, five or four? Over the past ten years, a period encompassing the 2008–2009 Great Recession, the after-tax difference between my tax-free investments and my taxable, moderately aggressive investments has been relatively small, only a percent or two per year on average. But a one-percent difference, compounded over many years, makes a real difference.

For just one of many examples, one of my favorite set-it-and-forget funds, Fidelity's Spartan Extended Market Index Fund, had an annualized return of 10.62 percent for the ten years ending June 30, 2013. (Past performance does not guarantee future results.) If you had been in that fund and had to give half back to the tax man (that really only happens if you have a lackadaisical tax accountant), you ended up with around 5.3 percent. For the same period, Fidelity's Municipal Bond Fund returned 4.3 percent. Yes, a difference of one percent.

That's why, for me, it seems clear that a *net five* is better than a tax-free four. Yet I have spoken to too many investors who never see it that way. They look only at the fact that one investment makes you pay taxes and the other does not.

There is no question that taxes can and ought to be considered as part of your overall investment strategy, but don't let them blind you to other, possibly better and more appropriate investments. Focus on after-tax returns, not the taxes you might pay.

A DOUBTFUL DEDUCTION

A slight digression. As a young man, I remember hearing about "shrewd" investors who would buy a failing restaurant or laundry or car wash because they "needed deductions." I never understood the logic behind that, but I was not then, nor am I now, a tax expert, so I just assumed I was simply too naïve about the tax laws to appreciate this clever tax-avoidance strategy.

Well, guess what? I'm decades older now, with a lifetime of dealing with money matters behind me, and I still don't get it. And when I do talk to people who know far more about it than I do, the mystery remains—and they don't get it either.

Here's how I see it: If I earn an extra $10,000 this year, I owe, say, 40 percent of that to the tax man. That means I am left with $6,000 in my pocket that I didn't have last year. That's good.

On the other hand, if I put that same extra $10,000 into a Betamax recycling franchise and the business goes kaput, yes, I do get the joy of a deduction. So I deduct $10,000 from my taxable income. But now I have neither the $10,000 nor $6,000. My $10,000 has become zero dollars. That can't be good.

As I said, I don't get it. Yet every day, people across America take steps, often drastic steps, to avoid paying the tax man.

Getting back to stock and bond market investing, my advice is simple:

Paying attention to tax consequences is wise, but *don't let the tax "tail" wag the dog.*

THE BEST TAX BREAKS FOR MOST INVESTORS

There are certain tax breaks that every American should take advantage of, including three of the greatest tax breaks ever offered by the federal government:

1. 401(k)s and IRAs

Get into your 401(k) and stay there. This is a no-brainer. If your company offers a 401(k) plan, you should take full advantage of it. Not only does a 401(k) plan give you the opportunity to reduce your current year taxes, it also gives you the chance to build your retirement portfolio tax-sheltered until you begin to withdraw your funds.

On top of that, many companies offer some type of matching contribution that will add to the total amount of money set aside for your retirement. It's free money—which is one of the rarest commodities in the world today. There is really no downside to investing in a 401(k) plan—provided the money is invested wisely.

In fact, many companies have adopted an automatic enrollment option for their employees, a development I strongly endorse. Unless you opt out of the 401(k) program, you will automatically be enrolled, with a certain percentage of your salary automatically withdrawn for investment in the plan. In the past, too many employees failed to take advantage of these plans. As the future viability of Social Security becomes more suspect, a 401(k) plan can mean the difference between security and a bleak retirement for millions of Americans.

But there is one factor that you should be aware of with 401(k) plans—plan providers are notorious for hiding the true costs of their plans. For instance, you may have been led to believe that your company's 401(k) plan is "free," but in reality nothing from the big financial firms is truly free.

The largest providers of 401(k)s—the major insurance companies and brokerage firms—have structured their fees in ways that make it difficult for many businesses to know the true cost of their retirement plans. For example, they may use so-called "no-load" funds that have higher expense ratios than similar funds, and the difference is sent back to the broker or some other person or place as a form of "revenue sharing."

Regulations that took effect in 2012 were designed to make it harder for 401(k) fees to be obscured, but in my opinion, there is still plenty of intentional obfuscation. Most firms are not vigilant about ferreting out hidden fees, so it may be up to you and your fellow employees to figure out what you are truly paying for your 401(k) plan.

If you happen to be in a position where you can help decide which plan provider will hold your firm's 401(k), please do your homework and shop around for a good plan at a fair cost.

Take advantage of IRAs. If your company doesn't offer a 401(k) plan, then you should be putting as much money as possible into an Individual Retirement Account (IRA), which offers the same type of tax benefits as a 401(k) plan. In fact, even if you are investing in a 401(k) plan, you may have additional savings you can invest in an IRA. There are different types of IRAs. Pick the one that's right for you:

Traditional IRAs. With a Traditional IRA, you can put away up to $5,500 a year (as of 2013) or up to $6,500 if you are age fifty or older by the end of the calendar year. You don't have to invest the maximum if you can't afford it, but every dollar you put into an IRA can be deducted from your taxable income for that year. Your tax-deductible contribution is phased out if you're married filing jointly and your adjusted gross income is more than $95,000 but less than $115,000, or if you are single or head of household and your adjusted gross income is more than $59,000 but less than $69,000.

The other advantage of a traditional IRA is that the money in your account grows tax-free until you begin to withdraw it upon your retirement (there's a 10 percent penalty if you begin withdrawing the money before you are fifty-nine-and-a-half years old). At that point, any money you withdraw will be taxed at your current income tax rate.

There are no income restrictions on IRAs. Anyone can contribute, although you can't contribute more than your adjusted gross income. So if you only made $5,000, for instance, then you are prohibited from contributing more than $5,000. There are some restrictions for individuals who also participate in a retirement plan at work.

Check with a competent tax advisor.

Roth IRA. A Roth IRA works a little differently than a traditional IRA, but it can offer outstanding tax advantages. The biggest difference is that a Roth IRA is funded with after-tax money.

The annual contribution limits are the same with a Roth as they are with a Traditional IRA. The down side of a Roth is that your annual contribution is not deducted from your current year income (because you've already paid taxes on it) so it does not provide you with any type of tax break for that year. But the upside is that, not only does the money in your Roth IRA grow tax-free within the account—as it would in a traditional IRA—but when you begin to withdraw the funds after retirement, your withdrawals are entirely tax free. You owe no taxes on the original contributions nor on any of the gains you earned since contributing to the Roth.

There are some restrictions on contributions for high-income individuals. As of 2013, if you are married filing jointly, you can contribute up to the maximum if your modified gross adjusted income is $178,000 or less. Your contribution eligibility is phased out if that income is between $178,000 and $188,000. If you make over $188,000, you cannot contribute to a Roth. If you're single, you can contribute the maximum if you make under $112,000, but your contribution is phased out between $112,000 and $127,000. If you make over $127,000, you cannot contribute at all to a Roth. (The income restrictions tend to change almost every year.)

Rollover IRA. There are IRAs that move your retirement savings from a "qualified" plan at work (401(k), profit-sharing plan, etc.) into either a traditional IRA or a Roth IRA. Rolling over to an IRA allows you to keep your savings in a tax-deferred vehicle and importantly, typically gives you a broader choice of investments.

2. Tax benefits of buying a house

Your house can be one of your best tax breaks. Interest paid on your mortgage is deducted from your total gross income, so if you pay $10,000 a year in mortgage interest, that entire $10,000 is deducted from your taxable income. (The alternative minimum tax may kick in. Check with a good tax advisor.)

The tax deduction alone may not be reason enough to buy a house. But it is certainly a great benefit once you've decided to take the plunge and buy a house.

Congress frequently debates the concept of eliminating the mortgage deduction in order to close that loophole and generate greater tax revenue. However, that proposal never gets traction because the elected officials realize that not only would they be giving up one of their own tax breaks, they would also be alienating the millions of home owners who might very well vote them out of office in the next election if they ever rescinded that tax break.

3. Tax Benefits of Stocks, Bonds, and Mutual Funds

If you want to take advantage of one of the greatest tax benefits available today for high-income investors, it is as simple as buying stocks and funds and holding them for the long-term. Stock and bond ownership is one of the least-publicized but most effective forms of sheltering your gains in the investment market.

There's no real benefit if you are a frequent trader of stocks—constantly buying and selling. If you hold the stock for less than a year, your gains will be taxed at your full income tax rate. But if you hold the stock for more than a year, your gains will be taxed at the capital gains rate, which is currently a maximum of 20 percent.

But the best scenario *from a tax standpoint* is to buy stocks or mutual funds you can hold for years to come. In fact, if you can hold the stocks for your entire life, you never have to pay taxes on the gains. Even if you made a million dollars on a stock or mutual fund, you pay no taxes on the gains until you sell (and even then, you would pay taxes at the reduced capital gains rate). If the stocks are passed onto your heirs, they inherit them at a "stepped-up" cost basis based on the date of death, so your heirs would not have to pay taxes on your gains either.

TAXES AND MUTUAL FUNDS

Taxes for mutual funds can get a little more complicated than individual stocks—and, as a result, they are often misunderstood.

In general, mutual fund owners will owe two types of taxes. You pay when you sell at a profit, and you are taxed based on distributions by the fund. Of course, if you sell for less than the price you paid, you will have a tax loss and no tax will be due.

What makes mutual fund taxes more complicated is that there are transactions within a fund that can affect your tax treatment—even if those transactions took place before you owned the fund.

For instance, if a stock fund manager bought Apple at a low price and then sold it after a huge gain, that price appreciation (realized gains) is a tax liability to all the fund's shareholders. However, if the fund sells a stock at a loss, it can use that loss to offset some of its capital gains that year.

THE BIGGEST MISTAKE SMART PEOPLE MAKE ABOUT FUNDS AND TAXES

In my opinion, the tax consequences involving capital gains distributions by mutual funds are often greatly exaggerated—or more commonly, simply misunderstood. For example, money guru Suze Orman once called mutual fund taxes their "whopping tragic flaw" in one of her *Money Matters* columns on Yahoo Finance. That comment reflects a view held by many other financial journalists and is certainly prevalent among investors I speak to. She wrote: "Actively managed funds have a whopping tragic flaw. When you buy actively managed fund shares, you literally inherit all the capital gains that the fund owns." What that means, Orman explained, was that you could invest in a fund one day and, if the fund made a distribution the next day, you would owe taxes on the distribution even though you hadn't owned the shares long enough to realize any of the gains. And that is correct. And it does seem to be a bad thing.

The failed logic of that explanation, however, is this: the price of the shares drop by the same amount as the distribution, which means you have less of a gain (or more of a loss) when you sell it. So from a tax perspective, this "flaw" is completely neutralized in most cases!

Here's how it looks with actual numbers. For the purpose of this example we're going to assume the stock market stays absolutely flat for three days.

You buy a fund on Monday. It costs you $10 per share. On Tuesday, the fund declares a distribution of $1 per share. That means they give you a buck for every share you own (if you chose to have distributions paid in cash—for most folks it's smarter to tell the fund to reinvest the dollar and buy more fund shares) and yes, you will owe Uncle Sam some tax on that dollar. But wait. On Wednesday, when you check the price of the fund, you will see it is now priced at $9 per share (again, assuming the stock market didn't go anywhere).

We used to hear from panicked clients—"Hey, my shares fell! What happened?"

Then I explain that everything is the same in terms of the value of their investment. They had a $10 fund, and now they have $9 in the fund plus the $1 distribution, so the total value remains at $10.

And here's what happens with the tax situation. When you eventually sell the shares, you will have less of a capital gain. How much less? It will be the amount of the distribution, or, in this case, $1 per share. Conversely, if you sell at a loss, you will have more of a loss, and again, that can offset gains elsewhere.

So despite what Suze Orman and so many others have said for years, when it comes to mutual fund distributions, it's simply a matter of pay now or pay later.

Avoiding excess taxes is certainly commendable, but not when it comes at the expense of smart investment decisions. But we all know that bad news makes more interesting reading.

There is one way that you can potentially reduce your tax exposure on mutual funds. Look for funds with low turnover ratios. If a fund has a turnover ratio of 10 percent, for instance, that means it is geared more to a buy and hold approach, so it would have fewer trades each year that result in capital gains than a fund with a high turnover ratio.

DO YOU REALLY NEED ANOTHER TAX BREAK?

If you haven't opened a 401(k) or IRA, it's time to start. There's no question about that. It can also be a smart move to take advantage of the mortgage deduction on a house and the tax savings of long-term stock market investments.

But beyond that, do you really need another tax break? As I mentioned earlier, some people buy tax-advantaged investments for no reason other than to save on their taxes with no regard for their actual return on investment. If you're earning millions of dollars a year, you may have a very good reason for seeking as many tax breaks as your advisors can send your way.

But if you're a typical consumer with a family to raise or a retirement to fund, you may not need another tax break. The premium you'd pay in lost earnings for most tax-advantaged investments may not equal the savings you would gain in taxes.

For reasons I find particularly perplexing, many investors—even sophisticated investors—are often drawn to tax-advantaged investments that ultimately have a negative impact on their bottom line. Sometimes those tax-advantaged investments make sense, sometimes they don't. You, or someone you trust, has to do the homework to find out the facts.

ONE TAX TRICK THAT CAN SAVE YOU MONEY

It's never a good feeling when the markets are down and some of your stocks or mutual funds have dropped below the price you paid. But there can be a silver lining if you choose to take advantage of it by "harvesting" some losses.

Selling some of your losers and using the proceeds to buy back into the market with similar investments can give you an instant tax loss and a new cost basis for investments you purchase.

If you happen to be sitting on large gains on other stocks or funds in your portfolio that have built up over the years, this strategy would give you an opportunity to sell out a portion of those positions to take some gains while using the losses from your other sales to offset the tax gains from your winners.

As an investor, you always hope to see your losses turn to gains, but if you play your cards right, you can have it both ways, getting the tax benefit while still participating in a market rally.

Let me offer an example: Suppose you own shares in ABC Technology Fund, and it's now worth $10,000 less than you paid. You could sell ABC now, lock in the tax loss, and use the proceeds from that sale to buy a different technology mutual fund that invests in the same type of stocks. One of the nice things about being a mutual fund investor is that there are almost always similar funds out there for you to easily do this type of swap.

Since the security you bought is similar to but not identical to the one you sold, you avoid triggering the wash sale rule, which bars you from writing off a loss on a security that you buy back within less than thirty days.

Finally, by sticking with your original investment idea, you avoid the mistake of letting short-term concerns cloud your long-term vision. If you buy a security because it has good prospects for five to ten years down the road, then a year or two of losses shouldn't send you running for cover. By selling one biotech fund and buying a similar one, you remain committed to the strategic reason you made the purchase initially. Yet in the meantime you get the tax advantage of what, hopefully, will be only a temporary loss.

You can use your loss—$10,000 in our example—to offset an equal amount of capital gains you take this year if you decide to sell out some shares of your winners. And if you don't have any capital gains, you could use the loss to offset up to $3,000 a year of income this year and the remaining $7,000 in future years.

Finally, a disclaimer: as I said above, I do not hold myself out as a tax expert. Do not rely on this chapter for tax advice. Every person's tax situation is unique, and getting good advice from a professional tax advisor is always a smart move.

Chapter 19

ARE YOU BUYING TOO LITTLE OR TOO MUCH INSURANCE?

There are worse things in life than death.
Have you ever spent an evening with an insurance agent?
—Woody Allen

Most of us approach the prospect of buying insurance with about as much enthusiasm as our next trip to the dentist.

But while many people actually overspend on insurance policies, the fact of the matter is that insurance is a vital and essential element of a complete financial plan. Without the proper insurance, you risk the possibility of losing much or all of the money you've spent your entire life accumulating.

You might be a wonderfully savvy investor, but life has a way of upending the smartest plans; insurance is there to help buffer the impact of unforeseen financial calamities. On a regular basis, investors see their nest eggs wiped out by storms, floods, accidents, health issues, and other misfortunes.

While the topic of insurance may not be directly related to investing, I have heard too many stories of smart investors who make dumb insurance mistakes and that is why we need to briefly touch on this important topic.

There are certain types of insurance that most of us would never consider living without. Health insurance, car insurance, and homeowners insurance are all standard fare for most consumers. Business owners might also seriously consider buying insurance for their businesses, and self-employed entrepreneurs may be well served to look into disability insurance—and, perhaps, critical care insurance.

But there are two other categories of insurance that merit further examination—life insurance and long-term care insurance.

WHEN TO BUY LONG-TERM CARE INSURANCE

With the average age of Americans continuing to climb, the demand for long-term care insurance has grown dramatically in recent years. Long-term care insurance can make your life much easier in the future and preserve more of your assets for those you leave behind.

If you live past sixty-five, there's about a 70 percent chance that you'll need some type of long-term medical care at some point in your life, according to the US Department of Health and Human Services.

Long-term care insurance pays for treatment of ailing individuals who need medical care over an extended period. It can help you cover the cost of in-home assistance, adult day care, assisted living services, or nursing home care.

Without long-term care insurance, you'll still receive the care you need, but it may cost you much of your savings. And should your savings ultimately run out, the state will take over the cost of your care, and may very well reassign you to a lesser care facility chosen for you by the state health care officials. Each state has its own rules on the specific income or asset levels required before government funding kicks in.

A good long-term care insurance policy will cover most of your living expenses so that you have a better chance of staying in the facility of your choice—and you can preserve your assets for your family or loved ones.

Long-term care insurance is geared to individuals who have assets they want to protect. If you are already near the poverty level, you may not see much benefit in buying long-term care—even if you could afford it. But if you have assets of several hundred thousand dollars or more, a long-term care policy will help you preserve those assets for you and your family.

On the other hand, if you have millions of dollars in assets, you may not need long-term care insurance. At some point in your life, if you do require extensive care, the extra costs probably wouldn't make a substantial dent in your total assets.

Naturally, the younger you are when you buy a policy, the less you pay. And that holds true for the life of the policy. If you wait until you are sixty or seventy, the annual rate increases substantially. In fact, if you wait too long, you may no longer qualify to buy long-term care insurance—or the escalated rates might make it highly prohibitive.

Obviously, if you are in your twenties or thirties, long-term care may not be of much interest to you, but as you get into your forties or fifties—and certainly by your sixties—a long-term care policy is certainly something you should consider buying.

LIFE INSURANCE

If you have a family that depends on you for financial support, you absolutely need life insurance. Once you have true *dependents*, life insurance is no longer an optional luxury. The question is how much do you need—and what type of policy is best for you?

Life insurance policies have become increasing complicated in recent years.

How complicated?

To answer that question let's turn to a column that ran August 5,

2013, in the online version of *Financial Advisor* magazine. The thrust of the story was that many financial planners steer clear of getting involved with insurance issues. Here is a quote from that column "Many Advisors Don't 'Get' Life Insurance" (emphasis added):

> When asked what was the most complicated part of under-standing and selling life insurance products and services, 37 percent of advisors said it was all *the different types of policies and riders and figuring out how they fit client needs.* A quarter of advisors cited "the abundance of paperwork required to sell and issue a policy," while 13 percent said it was the *"frequent product development changes."*

That's right. A large swath of the financial planner community threw up their hands when confronted with all the nooks and crannies in insurance products—and these men and women are financial professionals! So what hope do you have, Dear Investor, of making sense of the alphabet soup of different insurance policy options?

Let me offer a few helpful guidelines to facilitate your search. There are two ways to determine how much insurance you need.

The most common sense approach is to buy enough for your family to cover basic needs—pay off your debts, cover the mortgage, educate the children, and put food on the table.

But for those who want to do more for their families—and have the means to do it—insurance agents are beginning to push the concept of "economic loss." In other words, determine how much you would earn between now and retirement, and buy a policy that would replace those earnings. However, that can be an expensive option because, depending on your age, the pay-off for a policy like that could be well into the millions of dollars, which would require very pricey premiums.

A more reasonable approach might be a melding of the two concepts—get enough coverage to pay the debts, the mortgage, and basic expenses, while leaving a little extra to use to invest to provide an ongoing, supplemental stream of income.

How much coverage would that require? There is no uniform formula, but a typical working individual with a young family should have a policy of at least $500,000 to $1 million. Individuals with a bigger mortgage and a more lavish lifestyle might need more insurance—unless they already have assets in the millions, in which case they might not need insurance.

There are several types of life insurance products on the market, such as whole life or variable life (which build cash value while also providing a sizable death benefit). But the cost of those types of policies can be very expensive.

KEEP IT SIMPLE

My recommendation has always been to buy a simple "term insurance" policy for a set amount of coverage for a set period of years. A term policy is good for one thing only—it pays a death benefit. It does not build up any cash value no matter how long you hold the policy or how much money you pay in premiums.

So why buy term? Because it's a hell of a lot cheaper. You don't have to pay an insurance company to save your money for you. With just a tiny amount of research you should be able to find a term policy with the same death benefits as a variable policy but for a small fraction of the cost.

The money you save in lower premium costs with a term policy should be added to your well-managed nest egg. Over the long run, your overall returns could be, and I believe should be, substantially better with that strategy than they would be with a variable or whole life policy.

And never, under any circumstances, allow yourself to be talked into buying life insurance on a child! There must be a special room in Hell for the low-lifes who came up with that particular scam.

Chapter 20

WHY DO YOU BUY ANNUITIES YOU DON'T UNDERSTAND?

Some Annuities May Sound Like Magic, But They're Mostly Slight of Hand

So you think investing can get complicated? Ha. Try figuring out *exactly* what's going on with a "market value adjusted annuity."

Annuities might have a place in your overall financial plan. But all too often, they are marketed as a primary vehicle for your investment picture.

They are not.

There's a good reason annuities have become a popular alternative to traditional investments. They offer some enticing incentives—things like guaranteed returns, tax sheltered growth, fixed income stream, market-based returns, retirement security, and professional management.

But if you own an annuity, or are considering investing in one, let me ask you one question: Can you explain to me exactly what it is you own?

Probably not. And if that's the case, you are not alone. I've met very few investors who own annuities who can answer what I consider to be the most basic questions about what they own. Or worse, they tell me one thing, but when I ask to see the annuity documents, I find that they have a mistaken notion of what they bought.

It's not because they are dumb; it's because the industry, through either intent or neglect, has failed to adequately educate consumers about their products.

In a nutshell, here's everything you need to understand about annuities:

Let's say the annuity company expects the stock market to generate annual returns averaging 8 percent over the next twenty years, and that bonds will generate around 5 percent annually, on average, during the same time frame. (That's roughly in line with historical averages.) Everything they offer you will be based on those assumptions. There is no magic formula for them to earn more money. Therefore, they will then slice and dice those two figures (the 8 percent and the 5 percent) an infinite number of ways—partly to impress you, partly to confuse you, and partly to obfuscate the various fees, costs, and surrender charges designed to convert your money into their money.

So when the salesperson sits down with you to extol the wonders of the product he or she thinks you ought to have, please be wary. As I said, in my experience very few annuity owners really understand the terms, conditions, and stipulations of their policies.

Before you purchase an annuity, have the agent fully answer these questions:

- What is the potential for gain, the potential for loss?
- What is the guaranteed minimum return?
- When can you stop paying in?
- How long is the surrender period?
- When can you start getting income?
- What are the penalties if you need your money early?
- What if you stop making payments?
- What if you die?
- Is your return tied to the stock market, and what, if any, are the caps?

- What are your annual fees?
- What other hidden costs come out of your returns?
- What's the penalty for a lump sum withdrawal?
- How is that taxed?
- How is your money secured?
- What's the reputation of the annuity company?
- Are they solid financially?

After perusing that list, it's no mystery why there's an expression in the financial world that says "annuities are not bought, they are sold."

You, and investors like you, may understand how to buy and sell stocks, bonds, and mutual funds, but most consumers, on their own, simply wouldn't go to the trouble of researching annuities, comparing rates, scanning through the fine print, and deciphering surrender fees and return probabilities in order to buy an annuity. In fact, any consumer smart enough to make sense of an annuity policy on their own would likely also be smart enough to recognize that an annuity may not be something they would want to invest in anyway.

So if consumers aren't looking to buy annuities, then how do half a million new policies get sold in the US each year? They are sold because they are persuasively and persistently pushed by thousands of investment professionals across the country who stand to enjoy healthy paydays every time they close another annuity sale. For the sales rep, the annuity may be the most profitable packaged investment product ever invented.

NO MAGIC HERE

As enticing as annuities may sound, always remember that annuity managers have no special golden goose to make your returns any better or any safer than any other investment. The annuity companies are investing in the same stock and bond universe as everyone else.

In fact, every bell and whistle you add, every rider, every guarantee, every additional benefit comes with a price. The annuity company is there to make a profit, and they must take something from their projected returns for every single benefit they offer you. There is no other financially viable path for them.

Always keep that in mind: for everything they give, they have to take away.

And when it comes to the stability of your investment, picture a seesaw. The more upside of what they offer you, the more safe and secure your annuity, the lower the return you are likely to get.

The upfront commission for the agent and the firm that sells an annuity is sometimes as high as 8 or 9 percent. That means that right off the top, when you buy an annuity you're losing the equivalent of what might be a full year of investment returns from the stock market or several years of returns from the fixed income market.

In other words, if you invest $1 million into an annuity, your agent could walk away with a commission as high as $90,000. Not a bad day's work. And the agent may never have to lift a finger on your account again. Once the sale is made, the agent's work is done. And most significantly, your million dollar annuity has now shrunk to $910,000.

Beyond the agent's cut, there's a whole feeding chain of other people within the annuity company that you'll be helping to support with the money from your investment. The annuity companies get their share of your dollars through a complex and confusing web of ongoing fees. That's why they promote their products so aggressively to encourage financial professionals of all stripes to sell them.

Recently at my office I received a letter from one annuity company boasting that with one of their products, the agent could earn as much as $20,000 on a $50,000 investment. And that doesn't include the array of annual charges and fees that the annuity company and its managers earn. By comparison, if a broker sold you $50,000 in mutual fund shares, he or she would probably earn about $500 to $1,000 in commissions for that sale.

Are you beginning to see why annuities are a favorite topic when brokers gather?

And don't forget the ongoing fees that also drain your investment power. You may never know exactly what the total amount of your annual cost is because annuity companies do such a clever job of obscuring their fee structure.

One insurance company recently launched a new income-oriented annuity, promoting it as a low-fee product with only a 0.6 percent annual fee. But if you read the fine print, you would see that the company also charges a 0.8 percent annual management fee and, for those who are interested in some of the add-on benefits such as the "guaranteed lifetime withdrawal" option, there's yet another 0.8 percent fee. So you could end up paying total annual fees in the range of 2.2 percent. In the low fixed income environment that the economy has experienced in recent years, taking 2.2 percent off the top—in addition to the upfront fee—doesn't leave much left for the investor.

To be fair, there may be a good reason for you to consider buying an annuity. We'll get into the few benefits later in this chapter. But the simple fact is, with all the fees, commissions, surrender periods, and withdrawal penalties you could face, your long-term returns would almost always be lower with an annuity than with a prudently managed portfolio of stocks, bonds or mutual funds.

WHAT IS AN ANNUITY?

An annuity is essentially a contract sold to an investor by an insurance company that pays a fixed or variable payment at some future period. There are several variations of annuities—some come with immediate payouts, others with deferred payments. Some pay a fixed return while others offer variable returns. Some annuities may appear to be sold by investment firms, but in fact they are sold through an affiliated insurance company.

Despite all of the drawbacks, for some investors perhaps the greatest benefit of buying an annuity is that your money accumulates tax-deferred, just as it does with an IRA or other qualified retirement plan. But unlike an IRA, your contributions to an annuity provide no current year income tax deduction. So if you have money to invest, your first priority should be to put the maximum amount possible into your IRA, 401(k), SEP, or other retirement account. Once you've maxed out your retirement account contributions, if you still have money you would like to contribute to a tax-advantaged investment, that's when you might consider an annuity.

We'll get to the other reasons you might consider purchasing an annuity in a moment. But first let's cover the basics.

There are two primary types of annuities, fixed and variable. Here are features of each:

Fixed annuities

With a fixed annuity, you pay a sum of money to the annuity company in exchange for a guaranteed fixed monthly income for either a set period of time, for the rest of your life, or until both you and your spouse have died. Fixed annuities come with several types of payment plans. If you have a lump sum to invest, you can fund your annuity with a payment. Otherwise, you can pay into an annuity on a monthly or yearly basis for a period of years.

With a "lump sum" annuity, you can arrange to have your income payments begin immediately, or you can let your annuity sit for a few years to build capital that can be paid to you in monthly installments later (after your retirement, for instance). Fixed annuities tend to be very safe investments, but, unless purchased late in life, your return on investment is relatively low compared with other types of income-oriented investments.

Variable annuities

Variable annuities offer you more flexibility than a fixed annuity. You can have your money invested in one of a variety of portfolios (similar to mutual funds), including stock portfolios or bond portfolios. Some plans even give you the option of switching from portfolio to portfolio without additional fees, and without paying taxes on your gains.

You can buy a variable annuity with one lump sum or through a monthly payment plan. If you choose the lump sum option, you can either begin receiving payments immediately, or defer your income until later after the fund has had a chance to (hopefully) grow. When you do start taking payouts, the amount you receive with a variable annuity depends on the performance of the portfolio (or portfolios) in your annuity. (That's why some investors choose to have their annuity portfolios managed by investment advisors.)

That's probably the biggest difference between a variable and a fixed annuity—fixed annuities give you a guaranteed return rate while variable annuities, as the name implies, pay a return that can vary depending on the performance of the investment markets. Over a long period of years, variable annuities tend to outperform fixed annuities, sometimes by a wide margin. That's not surprising, since variable annuities are often tied to the stock market, and stocks, over the long haul, have produced greater returns than the bonds that tend to be the bulk of fixed annuities.

Some annuities give you several portfolios from which to choose. Your return is based on the performance of the investment choices you select. If you choose a stock portfolio, your returns will be tied to the performance of the stock market. If the stock market performs well over time, chances are you'll receive a much better return than you would with a fixed annuity—as long as the manager of your portfolio does a reasonably competent job of managing the investments within the annuity portfolio.

In some cases, your returns are not tied to a particular portfolio, but rather to an index that reflects the overall growth of the stock or bond market. If the market does well, so will your annuity—although your returns from an annuity will almost always trail the overall market. That's due, of course, to the layers of fees within the annuities.

For instance, if the market goes up 10 percent, your annuity may only go up 5 to 8 percent. There are sometimes caps on the growth you can earn in any given year, depending on the terms of your annuity. Most caps are in the range of 7 to 12 percent. So even if the market goes up 40 percent, your growth might be limited to a cap of 7 percent. Obviously, before purchasing this type of annuity you would want to go in being fully aware of these (sometimes severe) limitations.

It all goes back to what I said before, that the annuity companies slice and dice the expected stock and bond market returns in an infinite number of ways. If they give you a "benefit" in one part of the annuity contract, they have to take something else away. They can't get blood from a stone, so it's always a give-and-take process.

During a long bull market, the return on an annuity is likely to trail the market averages by a wide margin.

On the bright side, some annuities guarantee that if you don't withdraw your money early, you cannot lose money on your investment. So in a long bear market, an annuity could actually save you money. Over the long term, however, stock market averages are likely to dramatically outperform the returns of the typical variable annuity.

WHY WOULD YOU BUY AN ANNUITY?

Generally speaking, annuities are intended as a means to help fund your retirement. An annuity could be a useful tool in your investment arsenal if you meet one or more of these criteria:

- You want a guaranteed income, even if it means you may have to sacrifice total return. An annuity can serve as a security blanket in a diversified investment portfolio. If everything else fails, you'll have your annuity to fall back on. Best of all, even if your annuity company experiences financial difficulties, deferred assets from your variable annuity are "walled off" from the company's operating account so they are not subject to seizure from creditors.

- You plan to hold onto your variable annuity for at least ten years. If you expect to hold it for any shorter time period, you will probably be disappointed with the returns. Because of the high fees and up-front commission, annuities can take several years to begin building up a decent return.
- You're in a high tax bracket, and you've already contributed the maximum to your tax-deferred retirement plans. The money in an annuity grows tax-deferred, just as it does in an IRA, although you don't receive the current year tax break for your contribution to an annuity.
- You like the ability to switch your money from one type of portfolio to another without incurring capital gains taxes.
- You don't plan to begin withdrawing the money until you are fifty-nine and a half. Otherwise you can face some costly tax consequences.

WHO SHOULDN'T BUY AN ANNUITY?

I've already pointed out many reasons why all investors should think twice about buying an annuity. But there are several obvious factors that should make your decision automatic.

- If you haven't contributed the maximum to your retirement plan, then you have no business buying an annuity.
- If you think you may need the money in the next few years— or before you are fifty-nine and a half—you definitely need to invest your dollars elsewhere.
- If income taxes are not an issue for you, again, there's probably no compelling reason to buy an annuity.

In fact, even if you are in a high tax bracket, not all of the tax consequences of an annuity work in your favor. On one hand, your money does indeed grow tax-deferred while it's invested in the annuity, but when you are ready to take money out, your profits are taxed at your ordinary income tax rate—not the lower capital gains rate you may be assessed when you sell a stock or receive a dividend.

For that reason, annuities frequently are at a disadvantage compared with stocks. When you own a stock in a taxable account, all of your gains are tax-deferred until you sell (just as they are in an annuity). But the long-term capital gains taxes you pay when you sell your stocks would be significantly lower than the ordinary income tax rate you'd pay on the profits from your annuity. Bottom line is, owning stocks long-term can be expected to give you a better tax break than stocks inside an annuity.

Not only are the tax benefits better for you if you own investments outside of annuities, they are also better for your heirs. With stocks, mutual funds, and other types of investments, when you die your heirs pay no tax on the gains because they would qualify for a "step up" in the tax basis. But with an annuity, when you die, your heirs will have to pay taxes on your investment gains at their ordinary income tax rate.

Or worse, your heirs may receive absolutely nothing. Again, this goes back to the slice and dice concept. With certain types of annuities, you may get better returns but only because the annuity evaporates upon your death. The annuity company looks at the actuarial table and in essence, places a bet that you won't live longer than those tables predict. If you do live longer, great, you reap a bit of a windfall. If you happen to die prior to when the actuarial table says you will kick the bucket, they keep the money. It's all perfectly legal; it's in the contract.

But perhaps the best reason for shunning annuities may be the returns. After all, asset growth is why you're investing. If you want the best possible long-term return for your investment dollars, you're almost certainly not going to get that with an annuity.

HOW TO BUY AN ANNUITY

If after careful research you decide that an annuity is right for you, what's the best way to buy one? First, have a clear understanding of what you want in an annuity, why you want it, when you want to start receiving income, and exactly what type of variable or fixed annuity you want to buy. The more specific you can be, the easier your search becomes because you'll be better prepared to make specific comparisons on price and potential return.

You can buy an annuity through most life insurance agencies. Many investment companies also can put you into an annuity via a related insurance firm. My strongest recommendation, however, is that you avoid buying an annuity from a salesperson who calls you. That's a big red flag. Annuities sold aggressively tend to be loaded with fees and commissions.

A better approach is to call an investment advisor or insurance agent you trust and ask them about annuities. They may have some good options for you. But don't stop there. Go online and compare the rates and returns quoted by your advisor with annuities available online.

If you're shopping for an annuity, I suggest that you research the annuities available through a large reputable company like Fidelity, Schwab, or Vanguard. In my experience, I've found that those companies tend to offer some of the better deals on annuities. Again, compare the rates, including your upfront commission and the annual fees, costs, and possible surrender charges. Also consider the surrender period. All other things being equal, the shorter the surrender period the better.

If you buy a fixed annuity, you also need to be concerned about the strength of the annuity company. While the deferred assets from variable annuities are separated from the company's operating account and, therefore, shielded from seizure by creditors, that's not the case for fixed annuities. With a fixed annuity, your premiums go into the company's general account. If the company experiences financial problems, your annuity principal could be in jeopardy.

You should check on the strength of the annuity company through professional ratings services. You should only buy a fixed annuity from a company with at least an "A" rating or higher (such as an AA, an AAA, an A+ or an A++). You can get ratings by phone for free from several services, including Standard & Poor's (212-438-2400) and Moody's (212-553-0377).

You should also make sure the annuity you are buying will provide you with an adequate stream of income for your retirement. If your retirement is years away, don't forget inflation. A dollar figure that may seem sufficient now may be totally inadequate when you're ready to retire.

There are many drawbacks with annuities, and many reasons to avoid them altogether, but if you do decide to buy an annuity, do your homework and make sure the annuity you are buying offers the best possible potential for return at the lowest possible price. But probably the best advice is to make sure you understand exactly what you're buying. If you don't understand it, don't buy it.

Chapter 21

WHY DO YOU KEEP BUYING THINGS YOU CAN'T AFFORD?

Enjoy Life, but Keep Your Retirement Plan on Track

Being frugal is the cornerstone of wealth-building.
—Tom Stanley and Bill Danko, The Millionaire Next Door

We see it everywhere—people buying goods and services they can't afford. I see it among my friends, relatives, and very much so among clients of Weber Asset Management.

"A penny saved is a penny earned" is attributed (probably incorrectly) to Benjamin Franklin. Earlier versions go back hundreds of years. Regardless of who said it, the message is precisely on-target: money you don't spend is money you can invest for your future.

Put more bluntly, you cannot invest what you don't have.

If you find that you can't save any money—or at least not enough to stay on pace with your investment objectives—you have two choices: spend less or make more. Or both.

You might think that if you just made more money, saving would be easy. But people tend to spend to the level of their earnings—or beyond. You probably have heard that a surprisingly high percentage of professional athletes who make tens of millions of dollars during their careers are broke or bankrupt within a few years—or in some cases within a few months—of their retirement. Lottery winners have been known to lose their fortunes. Many other individuals have blown generous inheritances, bonuses, or the proceeds from the sale of their businesses. Part of the problem often can be traced to the siren call of extravagant indulgences.

On the other hand, you occasionally see the stories of cleaning ladies or handymen who manage to save enough to leave a million dollars to their church or charity.

The problem is not with making money—it's having the discipline to save more of the money you make.

Spending less and saving more can require a sacrifice in the present for a better life in the future. Regardless of how much money you make, if you're going to build wealth, you need to develop a savings mentality.

The challenge most of us face with money is that it's so much more fun to spend than to save. It seems that there are always more things you "need"—new clothes or home furnishings, a boat, an ATV, a better car, a night out, a tropical vacation. A boring trip to your bank to drop off your next deposit just doesn't compare. But the fact is, you can still have the things in life you enjoy—in moderation and in due time. First, however, you need to give yourself a solid financial foundation and the peace of mind that comes with it.

Now I know it's easy for me to pontificate about how you should save more. You've probably been hearing some form of that admonition for most of your life. Whole books have been written on this topic, and I don't want to repeat what they say.

Instead, let me offer just a few specific tips.

First, let's look at the biggest single purchase—and largest single investment—you are likely to make: your house.

BUYING A HOUSE

Much of the blame for the 2008–2009 Great Recession points to the huge number of Americans who were lured by easy money into buying homes they could not afford. Banks and mortgage companies greased the skids by allowing home purchasers to commit to loans far larger than could be supported by their incomes.

Don't ever let that happen to you. Yes, a home is likely to be a good investment if you stay in it for many years, but first and foremost it is . . . YOUR HOME! You cannot gamble in any way with the roof and walls that protect you and your family.

Rules of thumb are clichés and are often old-wives tales, but sometimes they are right. There's one particular rule of thumb I endorse that is often quoted by investment magazines and financial gurus: Mortgage payments should constitute no more than 30 percent of your net income, that is, your income after you have paid all your taxes. And that payment should include any property taxes, association fees, and other fees related to the ownership of your home.

Please consider that 30 percent to be a maximum figure. Anything over that and you are truly tempting fate. Put pencil to paper and determine what *your* 30 percent is, and then, when the real estate broker shows you a McMansion that is above that figure, walk away. Do it politely, but walk away.

Mortgages come in many flavors, and I won't get into all the variations except to say that I am a fan of fixed rate mortgages. Those allow you to accurately cobble together a budget. Variable rate mortgages leave you vulnerable to higher monthly bills at times when you potentially may be least able to afford them.

BUYING A CAR

When it comes to figuring out if you can afford that shiny new set of wheels you've been drooling over, the rule of thumb is this: if you can't pay off the car in around five years, you can't afford it. Sorry.

That Honda Prelude may not be a chick magnet, but it is safe and reliable, and if that's what you can comfortably pay off in half a decade, then that's what you should get. Or something similar.

Don't forget that the minute you drive a new car off the lot, you've just cost yourself several thousand dollars thanks to depreciation. If you're hoping to save more money, slightly used cars are a much better value.

A WORD ABOUT CREDIT CARD DEBT

Those shiny pieces of plastic are magic. You wave it past a credit card reader, and people hand you toys and jewelry and fifty-inch flat-screen TVs.

Except, the magic wears off quickly. The bill for that magic comes monthly, and woe to the investor who does not have the habit of paying off the bill in its entirety.

Some people, especially young people, harbor the magical thinking that they can keep debt going forever. Technically, they can, but in almost all cases credit card debt becomes a financial sinkhole. There is a reason credit card companies advertise heavily. Your loss— that is, the interest you pay them for the convenience of using their card—is their enormous gain. They count on the fact that a certain percentage of their customers will not pay off their bills monthly. That is fine for other people—but not you!

If you find yourself on a treadmill of revolving debt, do everything you can to get off. Pay off your debt as quickly as possible and then resolve to ALWAYS pay your monthly credit card bill in full.

Some folks think that it's a smart idea to keep a healthy stash of cash in a bank account rather than pay off their credit card debt. That's not smart. You will be earning much less from that bank than the credit card firm will be charging you, so over the long haul it makes no financial sense.

AN EXPENSIVE ITEM BECOMES MORE EXPENSIVE IF . . .

You lose your job. Or your spouse loses his job. Or medical bills pile up faster than you could have imagined. Or . . .

In life, as in the stock market, the future is unknowable. If you have allowed yourself to buy unnecessary luxury items when you are flush, you may have deep regrets about those expenditures down the road when life takes its inevitable dips.

The only constant is change. Think about that trite little saying whenever you consider buying something that is only a temporary feel good.

Don't get me wrong. Enjoy life. But enjoy life prudently and with an eye to your financial future.

SNL GETS IT RIGHT

And finally on this topic, a lighthearted look back.

In a classic skit from *Saturday Night Live*, Steve Martin and Amy Poehler play a truly clueless couple, sitting at their kitchen table puzzling over their finances. In this mock-TV commercial, a "salesman" suddenly appears in the room and urges them to get his "unique new program for managing your debt." It's called, 'Don't Buy Stuff You Cannot Afford.'"

Steve and Amy appear perplexed as they desperately try to comprehend this strange new concept. It's played for laughs but, of course, it is a distillation of the mind-set of way too many Americans.

The skit ends with the salesman saying . . .

"So, get out of debt now. Write for your free copy of 'Don't Buy Stuff You Cannot Afford.' And, if you order now, you'll also receive, 'Seriously, If You Don't Have the Money, Don't Buy It' along with a twelve month subscription to 'Stop Buying Stuff' magazine. Order today."

If only we could get those publications into everyone's hands.

Part 6

THE PATH AHEAD

Chapter 22

WHY ARE YOU BUYING STOCKS AND BONDS INSTEAD OF MUTUAL FUNDS?

A Better Solution Than Individual Securities

In earlier chapters I laid out many of the pitfalls of investing in individual stocks. I talked about the problems of finding good stocks for the long-term, the difficulty of timing the market, the challenge of overcoming your emotions, and the all-consuming commitment required to stay current with the market and your holdings.

Most people simply can't devote the time and energy necessary to invest in individual stocks—and those who do have the time are rarely skilled enough in stock analysis to invest successfully.

So what else can you do? How can you eliminate all the pitfalls of stock market investing while still participating in the growth of the market?

There's an easy answer: buy mutual funds. In this chapter, I'll tell you what you need to know in order to invest intelligently in mutual funds.

A mutual fund is nothing more than a basket of individual stocks or bonds, and there are two main reasons for you to put the bulk of your nest egg into good quality mutual funds: 1) instant diversification, and 2) non-stop professional management.

You want diversification because every stock is vulnerable to unexpected disastrous news; a new product flops, a manufacturing facility explodes, the CEO has run off to Bora Bora with his mistress—the list of potential disasters is endless. You cannot take the chance that one or two clunkers drag down your entire portfolio.

If you were to buy individual stocks, at a minimum you want ten different stocks in ten different industries. Buying twenty stocks makes much more sense. But then, of course, you have to continually monitor all those companies, and the industries they are in. Are you equipped to do that? Forever?

Probably not. That's why you want a proven professional manager watching over your stocks; every mutual fund has a manager or team of managers who watch over the investments inside the fund. (Yes, even index funds have managers.)

Simple, convenient, and diversified, mutual funds provide an excellent way to invest in the stock (or bond) market without the time and hassle of poring over earnings reports, balance sheets, and management summaries. Mutual funds are investments that hold positions in dozens of individual stocks or bonds. Some funds are broad-based and include stocks across a wide range of industries. Others focus on a particular sector, type of stock, or geographic region.

Whatever your preference, it's a lot easier to invest in a mutual fund than to do all the research and buying and selling yourself.

The convenience of mutual funds does, however, come with a price. That price may be high or low, depending on how you purchased the fund (you'll almost always pay more if you buy a fund through a broker). And with just a little bit of easy-to-do research, you can ensure that you don't get ripped off by buying a high-cost fund.

Also, you might be assessed a fee to buy the fund, known as a "load." In most cases, the load is assessed up front when you buy the fund. Those are known as front-end loads. But in some cases, you pay the load when you sell the fund. Those are, yes, back-end load funds. Loads may cost you as much as 3, 4 even up to 8 percent of the money you invest. So if you put up $10,000 to invest in a fund with a 5 percent load, your fee would be $500, leaving you with $9,500 invested in the fund.

But the funds I'm going to focus on here are known as "no-load" funds because they have neither a front-end nor a back-end load. As with every type of mutual fund you will pay the annual management fee for a no-load fund (that fee, knows as the expense ratio, is taken out internally, so you never actually see a specific charge for it), but there is no charge to buy the fund. Therefore, if you contribute $10,000 to a no-load fund, the entire $10,000 will be invested in the fund.

This is a good time to point out that brokers or other financial professionals may tout a fund that's "perfect for you!" And they will say, with a straight face, "Sure, it's a no-load fund!" That might be technically true in the sense that there is no overt fee to purchase or sell that fund.

Here's why that could be a bit of a slimy deception. All funds have an "expense ratio." That is the total amount of expenses that the people running the fund charge to do what they do—research, buying and selling, printing the prospectus, promoting the fund, paying salaries, hiring lawyers to ensure the fund follows SEC regulations, etc.

Wait. Did you catch that? Yes, buried in the expense ratio are promotional costs, and at some funds that is a very small number, but at others, that number might be considerably higher because the fund manager does some "revenue sharing." That is, they send some of your investment back to the person who sold you the fund, and that can make the expense ratio higher. Sometimes, a lot higher.

So yes, those brokers might not technically be lying about a fund being a no-load fund, but to my mind they are smearing the truth—and affecting your bottom line.

FINDING A GOOD FUND

Finding a good no-load mutual fund can be ridiculously easy. Thanks to the Internet and ever-more sophisticated websites, it is a process that takes minutes. Less than ten minutes, for many people. Yes, kids, in my day the process was laborious and paper-based. And what's worse, that paper was frequently outdated by the time I received it.

But all that has joined the floppy disk in the scrap heap of nostalgia. Here's what you do to find a great fund. Two simple steps.

Step 1. Go to a website of one of the major discount brokerage firms.

There are a number of good discount brokers on the Internet, such as schwab.com, fidelity.com, TDameritrade.com, or, for a totally independent perspective, finance.yahoo.com or Morningstar.com.

These sites all offer various types of fund screeners. That is, they each give you a different way to search for a mutual fund based on your criteria.

Using fidelity.com, for example, you would see up towards the top of the home screen is a tab for "Research." Click that and then click "Mutual Funds." You are now on the fund screening page.

With Morningstar.com, you click "Funds," then "Screener," then "Basic Fund Screener."

Each site is different, and sites change, so you may need to poke around a bit.

Step 2. Enter your criteria.

OK, look, I've been living and breathing mutual funds for a long, long time, and I can describe all kinds of nerdy ways to screen for funds. (Sharpe ratio, anyone?) Instead, I am going to reveal to you what, from my experience, are the three most important criteria.

You are going to search for funds with:

1. Below-average cost,
2. Below-average risk, and
3. Above-average, ten-year performance.

Ta dah. That's it.

Screening on those simple criteria will weed out all the funds you probably ought to avoid while at the same time rewarding you with a decent number of excellent choices.

Yes, there are libraries full of scholarly books and research journals that purport to show why you need to expend far more rigorous effort in your search for appropriate funds. I used to do much of that research myself—and at our investment firm we surely do exactly that.

But for the majority of investors who want to make quick work of investing and then get on to other, more enjoyable parts of life, these three basic criteria will almost certainly give you peace-of-mind and will likely yield excellent long-term performance.

Let me explain a bit more about each of the three criteria.

BELOW-AVERAGE COST

There are many financial writers who stress *cost* above all else. Their theory is that you greatly increase your odds of success by limiting your investments to the lowest cost mutual funds. There is plenty of merit to that argument.

Shaving a little off here, a little there, from your nest egg, year after year, has a definite long-term detrimental effect on the final size of the investment. That's why it makes sense to seek out low cost funds. However, too many folks become fixated on *low cost* at all costs.

There is no need to go to extremes; however, you can find well-managed funds whose track records clearly indicate the fees earned by the portfolio managers were worth it.

A sidelight: One of the nice things about no-load mutual funds is that when you see the "Total Return" figures posted in a newspaper or on a major investment website, that figure is a *net* return, calculated after all fees have been deducted. A no-load fund that is shown to have say, a 10 percent return for the year 2013 means that if you had placed $10,000 into that fund on December 31, 2012, on

December 31, 2013 your account statement would show you now had $11,000. So whether the manager of that fund charged the fund 0.1 percent of the assets, or 2.5 percent is irrelevant; your account grew by 10 percent.

Yes, there have been mutual fund portfolio managers who charged over 2 percent per year. While that *may* be fine in the short run, that's a heavy burden for your account to carry over several years. To be blunt, you'd be crazy to pay that kind of fee for a long-term investment, especially since there are almost always similar funds with lower costs.

As mentioned above, a fund's costs are often listed as the expense ratio and it typically is inclusive of every expense that would be deducted from your position in that fund.

BELOW-AVERAGE RISK

Let me be clear about this up front—there is no universally accepted way to measure mutual fund risk. It's always a mathematical construct, and it always takes a look back at what happened in the past; a posted "risk level" is used as nothing more than a broad guide as to what is expected to happen in the future.

The most commonly used yardstick is called *beta*.

Now we are getting into math stuff and out of my comfort zone. So I've asked a man who's right at home with science and math, my business partner, Jack Bowers (he's publisher of *Fidelity Monitor & Insight* newsletter, Chief Investment Strategist at Weber Asset Management, and a former Hewlett Packard electrical engineer) to give us a brief explanation of mutual fund risk measurements:

> Beta looks only at risk that is correlated with the overall stock market, meaning that if a stock goes up and down twice as much as the market, it would have a beta of two. But beta does not take into account uncorrelated risk. That's

why gold stocks have a low beta score despite being much more risky than the stock market.

Relative volatility, on the other hand, considers all factors that have affected a security's price in recent years (it's usually computed by taking the standard deviation of monthly returns over a trailing three-year period, then dividing by the same for the S&P 500). Sometimes this risk measure is listed without normalizing to the S&P 500, in which case it is simply referred to as "standard deviation."

There is no perfect way to measure risk, because math can't easily explain the psychology of herd behavior, and because some types of risk are hidden, meaning they don't usually push prices around until something breaks. But thirty-six month standard deviation usually does a pretty good job characterizing stocks and commodities, and an okay job of characterizing income securities. That's why it has become a standard of sorts in the mutual fund industry.

Got that? If it didn't all make sense to you, don't worry. The heavy-duty math is all hidden inside the "Risk" calculations of the fund screeners.

Different websites may use different calculations, but in all cases it still is extremely easy for you: A higher number means that a particular fund has been, in the recent past, more volatile than a fund with a lower risk number. And in general, more volatility equates to more risk.

Don't forget, by the way, that you do not want to side-step all risk. Over the long haul, funds with higher risk numbers tend to produce better returns than their more staid, laid-back counterparts.

High-risk funds tend to soar during periods when the markets are going up, but falter, sometimes dramatically, when markets tank.

Every investor needs to find a level of risk that suits their particular financial situation. (Professional investment advisors can be helpful in ascertaining where you fit on the risk ladder.) But just as with bulking up your triceps, it's often a case of no pain, no gain. Prudent risk is a necessary evil when it comes to investing. Learn to ignore the inevitable roller-coaster ride of stock market investing. Better yet, remember that when the market falls, if you don't need the money at that time, it may in fact be a smart time to add to your portfolio.

ABOVE-AVERAGE 10-YEAR PERFORMANCE

The US Securities and Exchange Commission requires that mutual funds (and just about everything else in the investment world) remind you that "past performance does not guarantee future results" (or some similar wording). And that is true. The future is unknowable.

Nonetheless, while everyone's crystal ball is forever cloudy, we can all have 20/20 hindsight. That is, you always have easy access to a mutual fund's past performance, and you can use that information to help tip the odds in your favor.

One of the things I like best about mutual funds is that the fund portfolio managers are forced to stand naked to the world—their track records are out there for everyone to see. They cannot hide.

Speaking of performance, here's something that makes me crazy—there are financial TV shows that present their audience with the "Best Performing Funds for the Past Week." Why in the world would any investor want to know that? What would one do with that information?

A one-week statistic for investment performance is beyond meaningless. It's just plain dumb, but I guess they need to fill airtime. If and when you see that chart on TV or anywhere else, turn away.

Moving on from that nonsense, you more commonly see year-to-date (usually listed as "YTD") performance, or one year, three year, and five year returns, and often those numbers are annualized, meaning they represent the gains or losses you would have had, on average, in each of those years.

Those numbers are certainly vastly more useful than one-week, or even one- or three-month returns. However, for you, if you're looking for a good fund that you can buy and stay with for some time, I strongly suggest that the longer the look-back period, the better.

Ten years is optimal, to my thinking, because, although there are many funds that have been around for two, three, or more decades, if you filter beyond ten years you eliminate too many top-notch funds. Plus, I currently don't know of any online mutual fund screeners that go beyond ten years. Heck, many of them don't let you search past five years!

It's true that during a ten-year stretch the portfolio manager may have changed, and if you want to dig into that information, be my guest. But that information may not be quite as relevant as it initially appears, since each successive fund manager will be restricted to following the stated "fund objective" for that particular mutual fund.

In other words, when you find a fund that has posted above-average ten-year returns you can have some assurance that a basic philosophy worked, irrespective of the particular helmsman managing the fund.

DIVERSIFY ACCORDING TO YOUR RISK LEVEL

In the financial world we talk about "asset classes," which are, at their simplest, broad categories of investments. For safety's sake, you do not want all your money in one asset class. Instead, every prudent investor must diversify across asset classes.

At a minimum, I suggest you have at least four no-load mutual funds, one from each of these asset classes:

1. Large Cap US stocks
2. Small Cap US stocks
3. Bonds
4. International stocks.

("Cap" is investment-world-speak for capitalization. It is nothing more than the total stock market value of a firm. Companies like IBM or Apple are large cap stocks.)

Again, you can use the fund screeners mentioned above to find superior funds within each category.

It is my belief that most investors would do quite well simply by putting 25 percent of their nest egg into each of those categories. If you are comfortable with a bit more risk, you can tilt towards stocks. For example, if you are forty-five years old with a steady income, you might boost the amount in the domestic stock funds from 25 percent each to say, 30 percent each, while reducing the amount in bond funds to 15 percent.

And for older folks who are retired or very near retirement, it might be appropriate to increase the fixed income portion (bonds) by slicing some of the investment in stock funds.

Always keep in mind that, in general, the better the expected returns on an investment, the greater the risk. But in order to stay ahead of taxes and inflation, you almost always want to take on more risk than the "safest" investments such as money market funds or bank CDs. I put those quotation marks around safest because if you are earning 1 percent at the bank but inflation is running at 2 percent, you are losing purchasing power, and over the long run that is anything but safe.

How do you determine the appropriate risk level? That is an area where it could pay to talk to an investment professional. He or she will delve deeply into your specific situation, looking at your income, your age, your expenses, and your current investment picture, along with your past investment experience, and then match all those factors (and more) to your future financial needs and goals. And only then will a recommendation be made for an investment mix that matches your particular risk level.

If you would rather do it yourself, you can visit the websites of the major investment firms. Many have tools to help you determine the risk level that might work best for you.

Whichever path you choose, please understand that the task of determining your specific risk level cannot be taken lightly. I have seen far too many investors who were much too aggressive or much too conservative for their particular circumstances. The results, over time, can be devastating.

Once you have chosen your funds, be sure to . . .

CHECK ON YOUR FUNDS

But not too often.

No fund is perfect, so you do want to keep an eye on your investments.

How often? Well, my advice has always been to look at the stock market through a telescope, not a microscope. Both the stock market and the bond markets fluctuate. Volatility should be expected at all times.

If you have followed my advice about choosing good no-load mutual funds, I suggest you check on your funds no more than three or four times a year.

Surprised? Well, as I wrote earlier, you never want to chase performance. Every mutual fund goes through days, weeks, and months in the sun, along with periods in the shade. Allow the normal market cycles to work in your favor. And don't forget, if you followed my advice about how to screen for good funds, you are likely to be in a . . . good fund. It won't be good always, but if it did well for ten years, there is a reasonable chance it can come through a typical market storm relatively unscathed.

When you do check on your funds, run the same three steps you did to find your funds. If a particular investment no longer meets any of the three criteria you used (below-average cost, below-average risk, and above-average ten-year performance), it may be time to make a change.

If your account is not a tax-sheltered account, don't make any changes that would trigger any unnecessary tax consequences—unless there is a compelling reason.

Whenever you perform a periodic check-up of your mutual fund holdings you are likely to find that each individual fund no longer represents the same percentage of your nest egg that you started with. Some will be a larger slice of the pie and others will have shrunk.

Don't be fanatical about your initial allocation. If your 25 percent of assets invested in US Large Cap is now 27 percent, you can trim it down to its original allocation, but it probably is not necessary.

On the other hand, once the variance is more than five percentage points it is time to put things back into alignment.

THE ALL-IN-ONE, SET-IT-AND-FORGET-IT ALTERNATIVE

You can do all I've suggested above, or . . .

You know your business. You know how to fix bones, or build a house, or teach children, but maybe you barely know a stock from a bond. You don't need to. There is a whole category of mutual funds that, for extremely low fees, choose the stocks and bonds for you, and automatically become more conservative as you get older.

Known as *Target Date* funds, these investments are designed for those people who don't have a trusted investment advisor, and who don't want to become investment experts themselves.

Available from many mutual fund companies, these "funds-of-funds" have professionals picking the investments. But unlike traditional mutual funds which maintain the same objective and strategy for years and years, target date funds are designed to gradually move higher risk positions into lower risk ones. Put another way, they become more conservative over time.

Target date funds almost always end in a year, i.e., Fidelity Freedom 2020 or Vanguard Target Retirement 2035. The year typically represents a time in the future when you, the investor, may need to start pulling money out of that fund. As of 2014, Fidelity Freedom 2020, for example, usually has around 60 percent of its assets in stocks (both domestic and foreign) and around 40 percent in bonds and what we in the business call "cash," but what others call money markets. Fidelity Freedom 2050, on the other hand, is aimed at younger folks. It keeps approximately 90 percent of its assets in stocks, making it considerably more volatile over short-term periods, but also making it more likely to produce higher returns, over the long-term, than Freedom 2020.

Some of my favorite choices in this category are Fidelity Freedom Funds, American Century Livestrong Portfolios, Vanguard Target Retirement Funds, and the Schwab Target Funds. Do an internet search on any of them and you will get all the information you need to get started. The process to set up an account is quick and easy, and help is always a phone call away. Or stop by at a Fidelity or Schwab branch office, and let one of their reps guide you.

The reps at discount brokerage firms like Fidelity, Schwab, and TD Ameritrade are basically salaried employees, so I tend to trust them more than the folks at the major brokerage firms who may be swayed by the commissions they would earn off you. As I've pointed out in the section on stock brokers, no matter how savvy or experienced you may be, you have no way of knowing which broker you can trust. There are no "reviews" like you might read in *Consumer Reports* to point you to the good and away from the bad.

Whichever fund you consider, make sure the expense ratio, which is easily found in any report on the funds, is less than 1.0 percent. And be aware that most target date funds have a minimum starting investment of around $2,500. You can get into American Century's Livestrong funds with as little as $500, but you must commit to an automatic monthly investment of $100 or more. Full information on these funds can be found at fidelity.com, schwab.com, vanguard.com and americancentury.com.

THE ADVANTAGES OF FUNDS ARE CLEAR

To sum it all up, no-load mutual funds give you a) instant diversification, b) professional management, and c) the ability to easily make changes, all at a relatively low cost.

Buy stocks or bonds if you feel compelled to do so, and if you are certain you can follow the stocks or bonds diligently as long as you hold them. But by all means, please use no-load mutual funds as the core of your investing plan.

Finally, while this may not be absolutely required within the parameters of this book, it nonetheless makes perfect sense to include a version of the standard disclaimer you see within virtually all mutual fund communications:

Before investing in a mutual fund, carefully consider the fund's objectives, risks, charges, and expenses. For a prospectus containing this and other important information, contact the fund company. Please read the prospectus carefully before investing.

WHEN CAN I BUY STOCKS?

There are a few times when you have my stamp of approval to invest in individual stocks. Here are those times.

1. You already have more than 70 percent of your nest egg in top-quality no-load mutual funds. Preferably, much more than 70 percent.

2. You have been through at least one full-blown bear market such as the tech-bubble disaster of 2000-2002 or the Great Recession of 2008-2009, and you didn't panic and sell all your stock market holdings.

3. You acknowledge (to yourself) that you *must* do careful research before you buy any stock and that you must then keep up with every single stock you own, OR you must diligently follow the advice of a carefully vetted stock market guru, making all buys and sells in a timely manner.

If you cannot meet all those criteria, stick with mutual funds. No-load mutual funds.

Chapter 23

ARE YOU SURE YOU UNDERSTAND INDEX FUNDS AND ETFS?

What's All the Excitement About?

OK, so now that we've examined good old no-load mutual funds, you might be wondering why I have not touted the new(er) kids on the block, index funds and ETFs.

That's a fair question. First, some background.

Index funds and exchange traded funds (ETFs) are hot. In the past few years increasing portions of investor assets have flowed into these investments while fewer dollars have gone into traditional mutual funds. In this chapter we will look at both the good and the not-so-good aspects of these investment vehicles.

THE PROS AND CONS OF INDEX FUNDS

Index funds are simple in concept: Find an "index" such as the Standard & Poor's 500, the Russell 2000, the MSCI Global Index, or any of hundreds of other indexes for various segments of the stock and bond markets, and then build a portfolio that duplicates that particular index. Don't try to do anything fancy, just hold whatever is in the index.

The logic behind index fund investing can be stated simply: beating the indexes over the long term is difficult, so stop trying. By following an index you are assured of not doing worse than that index. Plus, because these are "passive" investments with no person or team getting paid to make investment decisions, the fees to run the index fund are usually quite a bit lower than a traditional, "actively" managed fund.

That's the good news about index funds and their close cousins, Exchange Traded Funds (which we'll get to in a moment). And if you follow the financial media, that good news is pretty much all you will ever see.

BUT THERE'S MORE TO THE STORY

Here, in a nutshell, is my iconoclastic view of index funds: they are un-American.

Calm down and let me explain. When you purchase shares in an index fund you are saying, in essence, "I am happy to be mediocre." Remember, by definition an index fund hews closely to an index, meaning it should never drop below, or—and here's the spoiler— never rise above the index. It means you are settling for "average." And if you listen to the widespread advice of the financial media and many financial gurus, you will settle for average forever.

Now don't get me wrong. You could surely do many worse things in your investing life than being average. But as an American to my core, as an American entrepreneur, I bristle at settling for average. We, together, built this great country by striving to be above average, even exceptional.

While it is true, as so many have pointed out, that most actively managed funds will eventually fall below their index, many other funds will deliver better-than-average returns.

Let's look at the work done by my business partner, Jack Bowers, who is the chief investment strategist for Weber Asset Management. He has been the brains behind his newsletter, *Fidelity Monitor &*

Insight, since 1985. Jack provides his subscribers with specific mutual fund portfolios, each with a different level of risk. Many investment experts (*most*, I would like to say, but I cannot prove it) claim that you can't have excellent long-term returns by using just plain vanilla mutual funds. They would add that it's quite ridiculous to limit your investment choices to the funds of just one mutual fund family.

And they would be wrong.

Here's why I can say that. The April 2013 issue of the widely respected *Hulbert Financial Digest* showed that among all investment newsletters over the previous twenty-five years, the average performance of the portfolios in *Fidelity Monitor & Insight* ranked first on a risk-adjusted basis. It also showed that during that period, the newsletter outperformed the overall stock market (as represented by the Wilshire 5000 Index).

That past performance does not guarantee future results. But it does show that sometimes hard work and a disciplined approach—with no attempt at timing the market—can provide excellent outcomes.

And there are certainly other newsletter writers, advisors, and mutual fund managers who have achieved market-beating long-term records. There aren't many, but they are out there.

PASSIVE IN NAME ONLY

Here's the other drawback that the proponents of index-fund investing never seem to address. Let's assume you decide to follow their advice. Great. Now, what index fund are you going to buy?

If you buy one of the original, and still most popular types of index funds, you will buy a fund that mimics the Standard & Poor's 500 Stock Index. But that is an index that gives much greater weight to the largest American companies. As a result, the top forty-five companies in the index constitute 50 percent of the index. So if you invest say, $100,000 in an S&P 500 Index fund, around $50,000 is going into those forty-five mega-firms.

And that's the rub. You ought not have all your eggs in that particular basket. Sometimes those huge blue-chip stocks lead the rankings; other times small or mid-sized stocks show the best returns. Sometimes real estate funds are the place to be, or international stocks. Now and then emerging foreign market stocks are the hottest sector, while other times it's global blue chips. And of course, during bear markets, bonds typically hold up better than stocks. Everyone's a winner during some period.

So what fund are you going to buy? Clearly you need to have a mix of funds because a non-diversified nest egg burdens you with too much risk. Now you need to decide which index funds to invest in, and after you make that decision, you must figure out how much of your nest egg to put in each fund.

And when, if ever, do you sell any particular index fund? And if you do sell, what do you buy with the proceeds of that sale?

Let's face the truth: at that point, while it may seem as if you are being a "passive" investor, you are making "active" investment decisions.

Do you see what I'm getting at? Despite the attractiveness of the index fund story, decisions need to be made. They are not simple decisions, and investors who approach them that way might be setting themselves up for trouble down the road.

EXCHANGE TRADED FUNDS

Since the early 2000s, exchange traded funds have begun to steal some of the thunder from index funds. ETFs are similar to index funds in that they tend to be passively managed baskets of stocks, bonds, or other types of investments that mirror an index—just as index funds do. And, as with index funds, ETFs have become an increasingly popular way for investors to participate in the stock, bond, and even the commodities and precious metals markets.

Until the rules were changed in 2008, ETFs were all index-type funds that were not actively managed. Since 2008, however, a few managed ETFs have been launched, but the majority of ETFs are still tightly tied to an index.

The biggest difference between ETFs and both index funds and traditional mutual funds can be found in their name—*exchange traded* funds are traded on the major stock exchanges just like stocks. You can buy or sell them any time the stock exchange is open, and just as with stocks, the prices for ETFs change continually throughout the day. Remember that with all other mutual funds, including index funds, you have to wait until trading closes for the day before the transaction is actually made, and everyone who buys the fund that day gets in at the same end-of-day price.

On the positive side, ETFs do not charge a load—neither front end nor back end.

But you still face a transaction cost—the commission you pay your broker to buy or sell your ETF—just as you would to trade a traditional stock.

Then, too, you can use a *limit order* when you buy your ETFs just as you can with stocks. (A limit order is an order to buy or sell a stock at a set price or better.) So if you want to buy an ETF at a dollar or two below its current trading price—or sell it at a set price above its current price—you can put in a limit order and the transaction will be completed only when or if it hits your target price. You cannot do that with mutual funds or index funds.

However, as with index funds, ETFs also have a few disadvantages . . .

THE DOWNSIDE OF ETFS

As I said, ETFs are bought or sold on a stock exchange, and that means paying a brokerage commission. So at the very least, if you invest in ETFs, be sure you do so through a discount brokerage firm.

But perhaps my biggest concern with ETFs, the one that I have seen personally with many people, is that it can also lead to unwise trading strategies.

Here's what I mean. The purveyors of ETFs tout the flexibility of these investments. You can buy and sell anytime during the day. So if the stock market is falling, you can sell *that minute!* And now you've basically turned into a "day trader," a person who buys and sells based on short term—very short term—price movements. (In fact, ETFs have become a popular tool for many day traders who prefer to trade "the market" rather than individual stocks.) But if you learned anything from this book, I hope you learned that trying to guess what the market is *going to do* based on what it is doing currently is a fool's game. Not only are you trying to time the market, you are trying to time it *intraday!*

I have seen—as I'm sure you have—the stock market die in the morning, only to revive and rebound before the closing bell. Those poor souls who fled the market as it neared its low point locked in their losses and missed the ensuing gains.

My business partner, Jack Bowers, is blunt about his distaste for ETFs.

He believes that managed funds have some very important advantages over ETFs. In particular, he contends that a strong research department trumps passive investing. Here are a few of his views from his newsletter (keep in mind that both the *Fidelity Monitor & Insight* newsletter and Weber Asset Management, Inc. are completely independent from Fidelity Investments, and that much of what he says can be applied to other leading mutual fund families as well):

> Fidelity's small army of analysts has always been determined to get the latest story, and get it right. Over the years, these workaholics have kept tabs on thousands of companies, putting in long hours to fully understand industry business models. In each sector, they know the trends, the competitors, the risks, and the major factors that influence the bottom line.
>
> This kind of proprietary research is easily able to overcome other less-important factors. Expense ratios don't have

to be rock bottom, because the money Fidelity spends on stock research tends to pay back many times over in the form of improved performance. High portfolio turnover actually helps when it's driven by research, because decisions are the result of new insights, rather than a reaction to being in the wrong place at the wrong time.

Jack claims that despite the comparative long-term success of many of Fidelity's mutual funds, the media has devoted too much attention to ETFs because the media mantra has become "low expenses, low turnover." Yet they have no problem with "managers who don't try to reduce risk or improve performance."

He believes the media has become blind to actively managed success stories like the Fidelity Selects (which are mutual funds that focus on a particular sector). According to Jack:

Part of the media problem is a focus on short-term performance. To fully appreciate the advantage of good research, you have to look back over a period of ten years or more. Not many ETFs have been around that long. At Fidelity, where sector managers appear to have the stock-picking odds skewed in their favor, the idea that investors should walk away from any fund with an expense ratio of more than 0.25 percent is almost laughable.

Rather than questioning whether it makes sense to have a research department, the financial press should be focusing instead on the return generated for each research dollar spent. Unfortunately, for those who have adopted the ETF belief system, the real cost of kissing off actively managed funds may not become obvious for years to come.

To be sure, ETFs can do some things better than mutual funds. These investment vehicles can purchase commodities directly, mimicking the price of gold, silver, oil, and other hard assets. It doesn't cost as much to start up an

ETF, making it possible to offer foreign country indexes and unique index strategies that wouldn't be profitable in a mutual fund format. And for better or for worse, ETFs let you use leverage to magnify your gains or losses—without any need to qualify for a brokerage account allowing margin and short selling. No question, this blurs the line between investing and gambling.

DO THE FACTS BACK JACK?

So, should all investors throw in the towel and succumb to the lure of blindly locking your nest egg to indexes? Or is the actively managed approach really the smart way to go?

The proof, as they say, is in the pudding. Jack attained his market-beating long-term track record using nothing but Fidelity no-load mutual funds. We do not know what the next decades will bring in terms of performance, but Jack's twenty-five-year track record shows that the naysayers of active management ought to rethink their stance.

Jack Bowers and I are convinced that while index funds and ETFs have some important benefits, they are not a panacea for all investment needs. They cater to mediocrity, with the promise of average. As an American entrepreneur, I have a hard time settling for that. I want more. I want better. I want the opportunity—at least the hope—of beating the averages.

Suffice it to say, based on my decades of working with mutual funds, I believe carefully chosen actively managed no-load stock and bond funds, within a well-crafted investment strategy, to be the superior option. They have the flexibility to adjust to economic and market forces in ways that index funds and ETFs cannot, and they give you the hope of reaping market-beating returns.

Chapter 24

THE ROAD AHEAD: SUMMING IT ALL UP

The road to success is always under construction.
—Lily Tomlin

I've spent most of this book telling you what not to do. Now it's time to change course and give you my best suggestions to help take you to that financial nirvana you've been seeking. As always, these tips and ideas all stem from my thousands of conversations with investors across America, people likely to have much in common with you.

TIP 1. SAVE. THEN SAVE SOME MORE.

This may be obvious, but still bears repeating. To paraphrase the advice about real estate investing—location, location, location—the three most important things you can do for your financial future are: save, save, save. You can't secure your financial future with hopes and wishes. You have to actually put money aside, money you have clearly earmarked for investments.

Every dollar you don't spend on non-necessities is a dollar that can grow over time. If you are in your twenties or thirties (and hey, you deserve props for reading an investment book!), putting money aside now for a future that seems far away can be difficult. But once you form the habit, it becomes much easier. Your later, older self will someday thank your younger self.

Trust me; I know that from personal experience.

TIP 2. KNOW WHERE IT ALL GOES.

How can you increase your savings rate?

I'm going to suggest a specific money-management action that you probably don't expect, and that you and most readers are probably not likely to follow. So why bring it up? Because it has worked for me, and I'm the laziest person around (which is why I've had my wife do it for us). But if you do as I suggest, your financial picture will be vastly more focused, and I think you will see a real increase in your savings rate.

The tip? *Record every cent you spend.*

See? I told you that you would rebel against that advice. But just know that many of the most successful investors do it, and you should give it real consideration.

Here's my personal experience with this technique. During our early lean (very lean) years, every evening my wife wrote down all outlays made that day in a yellow ledger. This, kids, was back in the 1970s, when a laptop notebook was a notebook on your lap.

Today, of course, there are better and easier ways to accomplish this task on your computer, including several free spreadsheets designed to help you track, organize and analyze your expenditures (search for "expense tracking spreadsheets"). It's easier than you think because so much of your cash flows are probably already recorded via your credit or debit cards. You get a monthly statement itemizing all of those expenses. For everything else you spend, just be sure to get a receipt.

Once you start doing this, the process will take just two or three minutes a day.

Again, I know that only a few of you will do this. But here's some advice from a man who knew a little about making money grow.

> Now let me leave this little word of counsel for you. Keep a little ledger, as I did. Write down in it what you receive, and do not be ashamed to write down what you pay away. See that you pay it away in such a manner that your father or mother may look over your book and see just what you did with your money. It will help you to save money, and that you ought to do.
> —John D. Rockefeller

Why record all your cash flows? Because most investors—most *people*—have only the faintest insight into how they actually spend their money.

It's a lot like dieting. Most of us either forget—or choose to forget—everything we eat each day, but writing it all down helps demonstrate in black and white how many calories we consume each day. Once you see exactly what you're eating, you can start to become more selective in the foods you eat. The same holds true with your daily expenditures. By forcing yourself to record it all, nothing slips by. Those little incidentals, as you will soon see, tend to add up to much more than you realized.

If you're not already entering your income and expenditures on your computer, the sooner you start the better. As I mentioned, there are several free software programs (and some low cost ones) at your disposal that you can use to get started immediately. For example, a program such as Mint.com (which was acquired by Intuit, the makers of Quicken, in 2009) is free, easy to use, and powerful. I like it because it not only safely tracks your accounts and investments, it can also help you find the best deals on bank accounts, credit cards, CDs, brokerages, and IRAs. You might also take a look at youneedabudget.com, which, while not free, offers a somewhat wider range of features.

The specific choice of software is less important than the decision to get started organizing your financial life. And yes, no matter how much or how little you earn, you have a financial life. Ignore it at your own peril.

TIP 3. STASH THAT CASH.

Assuming you are able to increase your savings rate, where should you squirrel away that extra money? First, you must have a cash cushion. The general rule of thumb is to maintain a rainy-day fund that would cover six to twelve months of living expenses. That money needs to be in a conservative interest-paying vehicle such as a bank savings account or an ultra-short-term bond fund.

How do you find a home for that short-term stash? Do a web search on the phrase "best rates on money market accounts" and you will pull up a list of several sites that can help steer you to some of the better options. As part of this search, you will need to decide whether you care more about getting the highest possible rate of return versus having this money at a local institution. It's a personal decision based on your lifestyle. If you don't mind dealing with a distant bank, you can probably eke out a better rate.

But don't stress over a small difference in the rates at this bank or that brokerage firm. This account is not your primary investment vehicle; it is a convenient and safe home for your short-term financial needs. So just do a little research, make a decision, and then focus on the bigger, longer-term part of your nest egg.

TIP 4. SIDESTEP TAXES.

Accurate estimates of the percentage of employees who participate in their employer's 401(k) plan are hard to come by, but from my experience, that number is too low.

Basically, everyone who can be in a 401(k) plan should be in that 401(k) plan.

If you have a job that offers a 401(k) plan, be sure to contribute the maximum amount. Not only are you squirreling money away for your future, but in many firms your employer will match all or part of the money you contribute to your retirement. It truly is free money, and frankly, it's just dumb to let it slip through your fingers. Looking at it another way, why would you let your co-workers receive better benefits than you?

And by the way, do not think of your 401(k) account as a source of money for a loan. Some 401(k) plans allow for loans, but taking advantage of that feature is a bad idea for several reasons. For one, if you find that you are unable to repay the loan, it will be treated as a withdrawal and the outstanding loan balance will be subject to tax at your current income rates *plus* a 10 percent early withdrawal penalty if you are under age fifty-nine and a half. That could hurt!

Then, too, because you now have a loan payment, you may be tempted to reduce the amount you are contributing to the plan, and that hurts your long-term retirement plans.

Plus, if your employer terminates the plan, the entire loan amount is due immediately.

Since regulations change with some frequency, I won't list the other negatives surrounding taking out loans from your 401(k) plan, but I will strongly urge you to look at other alternatives before taking this potentially detrimental step.

If you don't have access to a 401(k) plan (or a 403(b), which is a similar vehicle but designed for educational and not-for-profit organizations), be sure to put the maximum allowed into an Individual Retirement Account. Again, regulations change, so you'll need to see what's currently on the books. Just know that you won't be making a big mistake whichever one you choose. It's far better to have any type of IRA than none at all.

TIP 5. FERRET OUT TAX SAVINGS.

Don't pay more taxes than you need to. That simple admonition is far more difficult to follow than it appears.

A number of years ago, *Money* magazine ran an annual feature in which it took a hypothetical, not-very-complicated tax scenario to several tax preparers. And sure enough, after the various CPAs and other tax experts crunched the numbers, the bottom line "taxes owed" for this make-believe family of four varied greatly from one expert to another.

The American tax code is an embarrassment to both political parties, and every attempt towards significant simplification has been blocked by vested interests. As a result, it falls to you—and your tax preparer, if you use one—to be vigilant about paying what you owe, but no more.

If you can afford it, by all means speak to a tax professional, as each person's situation is different. Push your CPA or advisor to look for the lesser-known deductions. The money you spend for the tax pro can pay back big dividends over time.

If you use tax preparation software, learn to use it well. Don't rush through it despite the tedium. And finally, if you can't or won't go to a pro or buy good software, at least spend some time doing research online. The Internal Revenue Service website, **irs.gov/help**, is a good place to start.

Be sure to keep good records of your investments. As a long-term investor, you may find yourself selling shares that you've held for five, ten, fifteen years or more. You can either keep your annual mutual fund statements hidden away somewhere safe, or better yet, do as I suggested above—use a good financial software program. Of course, if you do use software, it's incumbent on you to either diligently enter all transactions, or better yet, learn to utilize the automated download feature many of these programs have. Come tax time, you'll be more than grateful you put in the extra effort earlier. In a taxable account, every mutual fund or stock transaction is a taxable event, so keeping accurate records is a duty that cannot be shirked.

TIP 6. FIND GOOD NO-LOAD MUTUAL FUNDS.

As I have suggested repeatedly, the simplest and generally most effective way to invest is to buy no-load mutual funds. They are cost-effective, they provide professional management and diversification, and they give you an ongoing position in the stock or bond markets, or both.

Finding a good no-load fund does not have to be an arduous task. There are numerous sites on the web, as well as financial magazines, which rate the funds for you. As mentioned earlier, finding a good fund (or funds) can be as simple as 1, 2, 3.

You are going to search for funds with:

1. Below-average cost,
2. Below-average risk, and
3. Above-average ten-year performance

Those simple criteria will eliminate the questionable funds while giving you a good selection of excellent choices.

TIP 7. MAKE IT EVEN SIMPLER BY INVESTING IN "TARGET DATE" FUNDS.

As I discussed in chapter 22, target date mutual funds are managed specifically to conform to your investment needs as you go through life. The older you get, the more conservatively your fund is managed.

Offered by many mutual fund companies, target date funds are "funds-of-funds" that are managed by professional money managers who select a portfolio of mutual funds they consider to be age appropriate for their investors. The advantage of target date funds is that you never have to think about them. As you go through life, the fund managers make all the decisions for you to keep you invested in funds that are appropriate for your age.

TIP 8. IF YOU REALLY WANT TO MAKE IT EASY ON YOURSELF, USE A GOOD RIA.

As a wise person once put it, "if you want something done right, get someone else to do it." Is there really a good reason for you not to find a good investment manager to manage your money? If you need your car repaired, you typically hire an expert. Need your taxes done, you probably hire an expert. So are you being "penny wise and pound foolish" by not hiring an expert to handle one of the most important aspects of your life?

Without a doubt, some people really enjoy managing their own money. Those are the folks who study investment strategies, stay current on the market, research potential stock or bond picks, and make their decisions themselves. Or they do as we suggested earlier in the chapter and build a portfolio of mutual funds.

And in some cases they do very well with their investments. But if stock market analysis is not something that gets your juices flowing, or more importantly, if you ever feel you do not have the required patience and discipline for long-term money management, you should seriously consider letting a professional help steer your financial ship.

TIP 9. AVOID THE MENTAL TRAPS THAT CAN SKEW YOUR INVESTMENT DECISIONS.

As I've discussed throughout the book, investing begins with your thought process. To invest with success, you need to avoid the mental traps that lead to poor investment decisions. Here is a quick review of some of the most critical traps to avoid.

- Don't let fear and greed dictate your investment decisions.
- Don't let your ego get in the way of sound decision making.
- Don't succumb to overconfidence—the investment market is full of landmines that can trip up even the most experienced investment professionals.

- Don't rewrite the past with hindsight bias. Nothing is as obvious in the present as it may seem later with the benefit of hindsight.
- Own your mistakes. Don't rationalize your losses as the fault of others. And be sure to learn from your mistakes.
- Don't swing for the fences with that one big opportunity. If that big opportunity fails, it could derail your long-term investment goals.
- Don't invest without a plan.
- Don't try to make up for lost time by switching to a riskier, more aggressive approach.
- Don't chase performance.
- Don't be tempted by hot tips.
- Stay diversified at all times.
- Don't try to time the market—the sharpest minds on Wall Street can't do it and neither can you.
- Don't let marketing hype lure you into spending money on frothy newsletters and tip sheets that you don't need. The more urgent and incredible the pitch, the more suspicious you should be.
- Don't throw your money at speculative investments.
- First, do no harm. Think and plan before you invest.

And the big "Do," build the core of your nest egg around excellent no-load mutual funds.

Sad but true, even if you diligently try to follow every bit of advice in this book, you will still make mistakes.

Investing involves a lifelong series of decisions, and no one gets it right every time. But if you adhere to the basic principles and advice offered in this book, you can minimize your mistakes and maximize your return on investment and your wealth. And that's what investing is all about.

Good luck, Dear Investor!

ACKNOWLEDGMENTS

Several smart folks helped shape my thoughts into the book you are now holding. I bow deeply to them all.

John Boyd. As chapters were completed, the first person I sent them to was John. He's the co-editor of *Fidelity Monitor & Insight* newsletter, a position he took on after a distinguished career in financial journalism. Getting a thumbs up from John for particular chapters or sections of chapters was like getting a gold star in school.

Jack Bowers, publisher of *Fidelity Monitor & Insight*, has been my business partner and friend for well over twenty years. He's also one of the brainiest men I've ever known, and his input was invaluable.

My friend Jerry Lefkowitz, who not long ago retired from a high-level position at a major mutual fund family, went over every page and made many of them better.

Kathy Daly, vice president at my firm, Weber Asset Management, has for more than twenty-seven years been the person who takes things I write, rips them to shreds, and after we argue because I know she's wrong, wins. Usually.

And finally, it was a pleasure to work with Gene Walden. Aside from his considerable experience and expertise as a financial journalist, he provided exactly the calm and steady presence I needed to get this project done in a (more or less) timely manner. As I write this, we have still never met face to face, but after many phone calls and hundreds of emails, I certainly feel we know each other well. Thank you, Gene, for your smarts and your patience.